THRIVING

— in the —

BARREN PLACE

How Trust in God Fueled My Journey

Through Heartache and Loss

✦ • ✦ • • ✦ • • ✦ • • ✦ • • ✦ • • ✦ • ✦

PAULA ROMANG

Published by hope*books
2217 Matthews Township Pkwy
Suite D302
Matthews, NC 28105
www.hopebooks.com

hope*books is a division of hope*media

Printed in the United States of America

First paperback edition.
Paperback ISBN: 979-8-89185-164-1
Hardcover ISBN: 979-8-89185-165-8
Ebook ISBN: 979-8-89185-166-5
Library of Congress Number: 2025931429

Paula Romang's book, *Thriving in the Barren Place: How Trust in God Fueled My Journey Through Heartache and Loss*, was one of the best books I read last year. I was on a three-day study break in a cabin when I read it, and there were times I was so moved I had to stop reading and walk around the cabin. At other times, I was so moved I stopped and prayed the Lord would increase my faith the way He did in Paula's life.

The account is what I call "earthy spirituality." Paula doesn't whitewash the pain but deals with it honestly, faithfully, and biblically. I see her living her faith as part of our local church family where I'm privileged to serve as her family's pastor. Reading the book, I was reminded there are still many good things in the midst of such pain. I encourage you to read this faith-extending account, too.

Dr. Ken Parker
Senior Pastor
First Baptist Church
Kearney, Missouri

TABLE OF CONTENTS

INTRODUCTION

In the Old Testament prophecy of Hosea, chapter 2, verse 15 is an amazing passage. It says this: ". . . and I will make the Valley of Achor a door of hope. . ." A quick check of the footnote reveals that the Valley of Achor was known to the original readers as the valley of trouble and suffering. How can the valley of suffering become a door of hope?

Those who walk lives of faith know our deepest struggles often lead to our greatest seasons of intimacy with our beautiful Savior. He is beside us in our suffering in ways unknown to those who have not deeply suffered. Fellow sufferers all about us would likely nod in agreement at these words, recalling their seasons of great difficulty. With misty eyes and trembling voices, they'd tell stories of our Savior's tender closeness in their seasons of deepest suffering or loss. Like me, they would tell you the deep truths they learned during those dark days in ways they would never have otherwise. Strangely, many will say they would never trade that season of suffering for anything in the world; the truth, solidified and proven by experience, is a priceless treasure. The way our desperate situations force our faith into acts of daring and terrifying trust transforms our suffering into a jewel. Yet, the season of pain and suffering remains challenging; our soul scars remind us of that.

Those who've walked hard roads will also tell you how they emerged from their season of deep struggle with fire in their bones to share their stories with others. Not to put themselves on a pedestal or paint themselves as special for enduring great trials, but to tell others that this life of faith is real–it truly is full of holy fire, just as the Scriptures say, and like the stories you've likely heard. Those who've struggled desire to leave a well-marked path to guide others on their arduous journey, giving hope and encouragement along the way.

So, like those who have also walked difficult pathways and lived to tell the tale, I take up pen and ink and bring to you my story. I have suffered, hurled hard questions to the heavens, and felt the crushing blow of loss. However, I also learned the truth–sometimes hard, often beautiful, and always setting me free from the lies that held me fast. I learned the truth because I had to; walking in truth was not the easiest path, but it was the right one. It was the path where He walked, so I would be there as well. His closeness was paramount to my survival,--and that is how He became the Lover of my Soul. Friends, I give to you my story, my hard yet beautiful story: ***Thriving in the Barren Place: How Trust in God Fueled My Journey Through Heartache and Loss.***

CHAPTER 1

DREAMS TAKE ROOT; DREAMS BORN

"Behold, children are a heritage from the LORD, the fruit of the womb a reward."

Psalm 127:3, ESV

"Your wife will be like a fruitful vine within your house; your children will be like olive shoots around your table."

Psalm 128:3, ESV

I grew up on a family farm in northwestern Missouri, the last of four girls. My parents were devout Christians and raised us to honor God and His word, the Bible. We would gather around our kitchen table early each morning for a hearty farm breakfast, Bible reading, and prayer. My dad prayed aloud, and then my mother and each of us girls prayed aloud in turn. For our Bible reading, we often worked through the entire Biblical text in small increments or read from the devotional *Our Daily Bread*. The truths of Scripture were woven into the fabric of daily life. There was never a time when I didn't understand that the family structure was by God's design and that children are a heritage from His hand. Scriptures from the Psalms and Proverbs taught these truths, and I embraced them as my dream at an early age.

My deepest desire was to be a wife and mother. I would be the fruitful vine, and my children the olive shoots. My husband and I would prayerfully and skillfully launch our well-honed arrows for God's glory. Our heritage would be deep and overflowing with God-honoring family joy. My kitchen table would be long, large, and laden with happy memories and delicious, bountiful feasts. From that laden table, my children would arise and call me blessed. Our lives would be full of His best blessings, and He would be pleased with us.

Though I couldn't have articulated it as an eight-year-old, that dream lived in scraps and snapshots in my mind, as dreams often do. The dream became a loosely woven tapestry of family joys, a loving husband, a large farmhouse kitchen, and children—always the large brood of children. Intertwined through that loosely woven tapestry was the truth of Scripture. Family is His idea. Children are His gift, blessing, reward, and heritage. I couldn't imagine a better life or way to honor Him. I nurtured and protected the budding dream and kept it safely tucked away in a quiet corner of my heart.

Church life and church people were an everyday part of our lives. Our farmhouse was often the host home for the Sunday evening afterparty following church services. The grown-ups congregated around the kitchen table, swapping stories and solving the world's problems, while we played hide-and-seek and other raucous chasing games in the fading twilight. The church families were part of our lives, and we were part of theirs.

As such, it was not uncommon for one of the families to bring us a bag of hand-me-down clothes. In one of those bags was an orange sundress liberally embellished with yellow rick-rack. The patch pockets were embroidered with yellow flowers. It fit me, and I immediately claimed it. It became my go-to outfit for everything from gardening to church. In my orange sundress, I was convinced I was a barefoot, sun-kissed vision, and as such, I went about my farm and garden chores.

Summers were full of the hard work innate to farm life. West of our farmhouse lay a half-acre plot of ground that served as our vegetable garden. We grew massive quantities of corn, tomatoes, green beans, and anything we could pickle or can for winter. My summers were spent in the labor-intensive, yet constructive task of gardening, preserving, and canning what our garden produced.

After morning chores, summer mornings were spent weeding the garden and picking whatever crop was in season. We often filled paper grocery bags with freshly picked green beans and hauled them to the kitchen for snapping. Hot afternoons were spent snapping beans as we listened to the radio. When Mom was home, she would tune in to the Christian radio station's elusive signal that wafted to us only with a favorable wind and away from us on a contrary wind. In the evenings, we could sometimes hear Focus on the Family. The speakers often spoke on marriage and family—topics of keen interest to me. I could listen to snippets of the speakers' messages, usually followed by a roar of laughter as the signal flitted away. Whatever those Christian people were doing seemed delightful, yet forever elusive. Yet, I wanted to be part of that world, hear the whole sermon, laugh with them, and be in on the joke that seemed forever out of reach.

As I pressed my ear against the radio speaker, hoping to hear another message fragment, another dream took root. Christian people taught, sang, spoke, and wrote books for a living, while others listened, applauded, and laughed. If I could do that, I could be part of that world. So, the sun-kissed, barefoot vision in her orange sundress took that seedling of a dream, tucked it away for safekeeping beside the dream of a large brood of children and a long farmhouse table, and refused to let them die.

***

By Christmas of 1999, my husband Mark and I had been married for five years, had purchased our first house, and were trying in vain to start our family. After two years of monthly disappointment, the only thing close to an answer was when one doctor referred to me as "out of phase." When I pressed further, he mumbled a non-answer full of medical terminology and was gone. Shortly thereafter, another doctor finally told me the truth. If I hadn't conceived naturally within six months to a year, standard conception was unlikely. He referred us to an infertility specialist specializing in vitro fertilization (IVF). I was aware of the potential ethical issues and listened to several Christian radio programs on IVF. I prayed fervently that God would guide us toward the right decision. I knew no matter the circumstances—whether we could conceive through this method or not—God was sovereign over all the highly technical medical intricacies along the way. He was Lord over whatever transpired in my body, in the operating room, and in the lab. Mark and I decided to move forward with the procedure at the beginning of 2000. We were presented with a timeline for medicine regimens, egg retrieval surgery, and embryo transfer; things began happening quickly.

Part of my daily regimen included giving myself shots. Certain medications were to be given in certain muscles for best results, and so began the daily ritual of giving myself shots in my thighs with a thin, short needle. My thighs were soon dotted with tiny red needle marks surrounded by purplish, marbled bruising. The date was set for my egg retrieval surgery. Mark drove me down to the hospital, and I went through regular surgery pre-op. We sat in the surgery waiting bay, surrounded by green curtains, talking quietly and nervously about the procedure.

Almost without warning, our doctor appeared in her blue and green scrubs and upbeat chatter: "Are you ready? Let's do this!" She indicated that the nurses would start my sedation and she'd meet me in the operating room. Mark was ushered into a surgery waiting room, my sedation drip began, and the fog began to descend upon me. The surgery techs quickly wheeled me through double doors and into a surgery bay where our doctor waited. She greeted me briefly and eyed the surgery techs. They gave her an affirmative nod, gripped the corners of the sheet beneath me, and began the countdown to transfer me from the gurney to the operating table—and I was out.

I woke in a surgery recovery bay, snuggled under several warm blankets. A nurse came, taking more blankets from a warmer, trading them for the ones covering me. She offered me a small cup of water and a saltine cracker. I sipped the water and nibbled the crackers, sinking again into the warm blankets—dozing in and out. I roused to see Mark approaching, a nervous, apprehensive smile on his lips. The nurse approached Mark with a clipboard, explained the discharge instructions, and marked the signature line with a highlighter. He signed the discharge papers, and the nurse handed him a plastic bag containing my clothes and shoes. Mark and the nurse helped me sit up and move to a chair, my limbs leaden and my head thick with the fog of sedation. Mark helped dress me—putting my feet into the legs of my sweatpants and guiding my arms into my shirt sleeves. I stuffed my feet into my shoes, and he stooped to tie them. Mark retrieved the car as the nurse settled me in a wheelchair and wheeled me to our waiting car. I dozed most of the way home and then settled on the couch.

Later that afternoon, the doctor called us. She had retrieved twenty-one eggs from me and was pleased by that result. The initial result of the petri dish fertilization was fourteen embryos. She expected to have eight embryos by the fifth day of gestation. She planned to implant the two most viable embryos and the rest would go into cryopreservation straws for further attempts if the first attempt failed. All we could do was wait for four more days until the day of our embryo transfer.

My mind reeled—fourteen embryos? "Lord," I said, "I wanted a large brood of children, is this how You intend to do this?" The number tumbled about in my head. I told Mark what the doctor had said and re-read all my notes for him. We moved through the evening in stunned, quiet conversation. We re-read my notes, and I rehashed what the doctor had said. Then we settled down to pray. We prayed over our embryo babies gestating in their petri dish. We prayed for the process and that the embryos He chose would be the most viable. We prayed they would all survive, according to His will. We prayed for the doctors, nurses, and lab techs. We covered the scenario in prayer and left it and our embryo babies in His care. As I settled into bed that night, the number fourteen still washed about in my head. "Lord," I prayed, "What are You doing? Fourteen babies? Are You serious? What is happening? What are you doing?" There was only silence.

Our doctor called us daily for a status update on our embryo babies. She indicated their numbers would drop steadily each day as we approached day five, the peak day for transfer. She was right. Their numbers dropped daily, leaving us eight embryos on transfer day. Our doctor could implant two and planned to store the rest in cryopreservation straws. I prayed over the ones who flew away, releasing them to His care. I prayed He would select the embryos He knew would develop into the babies He wanted Mark and me to parent. I prayed for His protecting and sustaining grace over the embryo babies placed in cryopreservation and left the situation in His hands.

Our embryo transfer was scheduled; it happened to fall on my birthday. We drove to the appointment in quiet anticipation. We were ushered into a special room called the embryo transfer room. I took the valium pill for sedation as instructed for the quick and minimally invasive procedure. The doctor met us there with her same upbeat smile. Before the transfer, she showed us an image of the two embryos they were preparing to implant. I saw two clear round bubbles on the screen—they looked like soap bubbles. We marveled at them, and then the procedure began—it was over as soon as it began. I dozed in the quiet room while Mark waited. When the nurse cleared us, Mark helped me get dressed. Once again, he retrieved the car, and the nurse wheeled me into the waiting vehicle. I was back on the sofa at home, as the doctor instructed. I remained off work and at a moderate activity level at home for several days.

Following the embryo transfer, I began another regimen of shots. This time, I was to give myself progesterone shots. They were to be given in the hip muscle. The progesterone was a thick oily liquid delivered through a much longer and larger needle deep into the muscle. I considered myself a gritty "getter-done" woman, so I readied the syringe, backed up to the mirror, counted down, stabbed myself in the backside with the needle, and slowly pushed the thick liquid into my hip. I did this daily for a week.

Within a week after the transfer, I had a pregnancy test. It was positive! I was pregnant! I would have blood tests and further pregnancy tests to make sure my hormone levels were heading in the right direction. I would also have a sonogram to determine whether both embryos survived or just one. The farmgirl in her orange sundress within me held her breath in guarded anticipation.

On the day of our sonogram, the doctor ushered Mark and me into the darkened room lit only by the computer monitor and an occasional beam of light from the hallway as the nurse came and went. Mark stood near me, holding my hand. As the doctor began the procedure, a murky black-and-white triangle appeared on the computer screen. She started her search for our gestating babies. I held my breath and whispered a prayer.

"There's one," she said. Pointing to a shadowy bean-like oval on the computer monitor. "Twin A!"

Time seemed to crawl as she continued her search. "Lord, where is the other embryo? Please don't let it die. Please help her find it," I prayed.

"Let me look around some more," she said quietly to the nurse. The doctor continued searching.

"Aha, I knew it!" the doctor said, laughing. "There it is!" She pointed to another bean-like oval. "Twin B!"

I was pregnant with twins! God had done it! He had preserved both tiny lives! God was finally answering my prayers with His characteristic abundance. I couldn't wait to see how His story unfolded in our lives. I posted the black and white sonogram photo on the fridge and began an early morning ritual of placing one hand on the sonogram image and the other on my belly as I prayed over our tiny babies. I prayed for God's blessing over their growth and development, for whoever He already knew they would become. I prayed for Mark and me to have the wisdom, strength, and grace for whatever challenges lay ahead, and I entrusted them to

His tender and sovereign care. The farmgirl in her orange sundress within me laughed aloud, twirling in the sunshine for joy. He had done it! He had done it!

My tummy grew, and I was visibly pregnant! I ditched the regular clothes for maternity clothes and basked in my motherly glow. We were scheduled for a sonogram at the twenty-week mark to monitor gestation and see the sex of our babies if they cooperated. At the imaging appointment, once again, we were ushered into a darkened room lit only by the computer monitor and the light from the hall. Mark stood nearby, holding my hand. The doctor explained the procedure and squirted the warm gel on my belly. The same black-and-white image appeared, but now the bean-like ovals had blossomed. Their heads, fingers, feet, and toes were clearly outlined. The doctor pointed out their spines—the "string of pearls" he called them. We watched their squirming shadows in amazement—we were having twin boys!

This was the fruition of the carefully nurtured dream. I was certain these tiny boys would be the first of many more children, and God was finally granting me the large brood of children for which I'd prayed. Children were His blessing to families, and I was certain this was just the beginning of His plan for us. The sun-kissed farmgirl in her orange sundress leaped for joy in my mind's eye.

Mark and I began choosing baby boy names. Several names were bantered about; we each lobbied for our choices. In the end, we chose Matthew Caleb and Luke David. The first baby born would be Matthew because it fell first among the gospels, and Luke would be the second.

As I entered the third trimester, I began having preterm labor. The doctor prescribed medication and bed rest. I resigned from my office position and went home to care for myself and my boys. Sonograms and doctor appointments were amped up to weekly appointments, and if I wasn't going to either a sonogram or doctor appointment, I was ordered to the sofa. The doctors were trying their best to get the boys to the thirty-four to thirty-six week mark to ensure their best lung development and outcome outside the womb. I was instructed to lie on my left side and drink plenty of water. I spent my days watching "chick flicks" and waddling to and from the bathroom. My mother came to drive me to and from sonogram and OB appointments when Mark was working. She also cooked for Mark and me and kept me well-supplied with hearty snacks. I dutifully lay on the couch, crocheting baby blankets. I watched the yellow and orange autumn leaves flutter against the blue sky while craving heavily buttered white rice or mashed potatoes.

Sonograms showed that Twin B had a significantly smaller, compressed umbilical cord, and his amniotic fluid was also low. The sonograms also showed that Twin B's weight gain was markedly slower. Our team of doctors closely monitored both boys, but especially Twin B. For a time, the boys were both positioned with their heads downward, signaling a natural birth was still on the table. However, from one sonogram appointment to the next, their positions changed. As the final trimester chugged along, the boys became increasingly cramped and compressed; however, they changed positions once again. Twin A was breech, and Twin B was transverse. A Cesarean section was our only option now.

I dutifully continued on bed rest. My bulging belly extended from my chest to mid-thigh; I could breathe in a semi-reclining position, so I gathered various couch and bed pillows into a nest. I sat propped in my nest, drinking water, breathing, waiting, and praying over my baby boys.

Following one of our weekly imaging appointments, the doctor was strangely quiet, his brows furrowed as he shook his head in frustration.

"I can't see much. The babies are so tightly compacted that I can't give them accurate information on Twin B. There's no way I can give them good data," he sighed deeply. I nodded. "I'll have to call your docs. When's your next appointment?" he asked.

"In an hour. We go straight from here to our OB appointment," I said flatly. He nodded.

"I'll call them right away," he said. "We have to make a plan." He excused himself and was gone.

"Lord?" I prayed as I prepared to leave, "Please protect these boys. Please help us make these hard decisions. Carry us, Father."

Our OB doctors met us with the same quiet concern and furrowed brows. They had spoken with our imaging doctor. Our boys would have to be delivered soon; we needed a specialist. They referred us immediately to a perinatologist, an OB who specializes in high-risk pregnancies, and scheduled us for an appointment that same afternoon. We would have to leave immediately to make the appointment at the downtown office. Mark stopped and got me a sandwich as we zipped through traffic to the downtown office.

At the perinatologist's office, we checked in and were immediately taken into an exam room where we nervously waited.

"What's happening?" Mark asked. I did not answer.

The perinatologist arrived, flipping through sonogram images and notes from our OB/GYN as she talked to both me and her nurse.

"When did you last eat?" she asked me. I mentioned the sandwich I'd eaten on the way downtown. The perinatologist nodded; the wheels in her mind were turning rapidly.

"Check the operating schedule for an opening," she said to her nurse. The nurse nodded and scurried away.

The perinatologist turned to us, took a deep breath, and began: "Well, we need to get these babies out. We can't get accurate data, and we're guessing and hoping for the best by leaving them in. If we deliver them, we're also taking a risk with their lung development. Either way, it's a risk. The upside to delivering is that we will know, and we have NICU." She paused. "I recommend we deliver as soon as possible." She eyed us both. Mark and I nodded in agreement.

The nurse returned with a surgery schedule. They poured over it, pinpointing possible times later that afternoon or the following day. They made their choice and returned with a plan.

"Okay," the perinatologist sighed deeply, "here's the plan. Mom, you'll need to stay here overnight. My nurse is scheduling your surgery for one o'clock tomorrow. I'll call someone to get you settled in a room. I'll see you tomorrow in pre-op." She nodded toward us both and was gone.

"Whoa. That's a lot," Mark said, as if to himself. I leaned back on the exam table, propped myself up with my arms, and breathed.

A nurse in pink scrubs peered in.

"Are you Paula?" she asked, smiling. I nodded. I lumbered off the exam table, waddling toward the door. "Oh my, stay right there," she said. She returned with a wheelchair and guided me into it. Mark scurried after us as she fast-walked us toward the elevator. On the maternity floor, she wheeled me past the nurses' station and into a room at the end of the hall. A gown and slipper socks lay on the bed. Mark helped me change and stuffed my clothes and shoes into a plastic bag.

Mark decided to go home for the night and return in the

morning. He planned to call his parents and relay the news. I would call my parents and church friends so everyone would be praying for Mark, me, and the boys.

When Mark left, I called our small group leader at church, then I called my mom. I relayed in detail the events of the day. I could hear her scribbling down the hospital name and address, my room number, and surgery time. She assured me that she and Dad would be in prayer, and would also come up for the surgery. She prayed with me, and we ended our call.

That started a long, wakeful night alone for me. I was not allowed to eat or drink due to the pending surgery. Sleep was not going to come, that was obvious to me, so I began to pray. I prayed as I always had. I prayed for the boys' safe delivery, especially for Twin B and his needs. I prayed for Mark and me as we embarked on parenting twin boys. I had no idea what to expect, but I also knew that God was already all over whatever lay ahead for us. My head pounded, and my back throbbed. My massive belly impeded my ability to shift positions without help, so I remained stuck in one position like an upside-down turtle. I was relieved to see the first golden rays of sunlight wash over the window sill. The morning activity began on the nursing floor. Breakfast trays were being distributed; a food service worker started to bring me a breakfast tray, and the nurse waved him off, saying, "Surgery today!"

My parents arrived by midmorning. I was glad for the company. I relayed what information I had and rehashed what I'd told them the night before. We snapped a few photos and chatted to pass the time. Mark arrived soon after. We chatted with my parents as the anticipation grew. There was nothing to do but wait. Soon, the doctor appeared and told us briefly what would happen next and that surgery prep would be underway soon. A nurse appeared with a gurney, and I was quickly wheeled away. Mark and my parents followed. My parents stayed in a surgery waiting area, and Mark came with me. Surgery techs worked promptly and efficiently, moving me from place to place. They sat me on a table for my spinal block. I was told to lean forward against Mark, a tech was feeling along my spine. He gave me a quick warning, then a needle poke. I was transferred to a surgery table, arms flung out, and a drape placed, blocking my view.

The anesthesiologist stood nearby and asked what I felt. I said, "It felt like they wrote on my belly with a marker!" He smiled and said, "That's good, because that's *not* what they just did!"

Mark was nearby, opposite the anesthesiologist. A team from the NICU stood ready with oxygen masks and hoods. A scale and other supplies awaited our boys' arrival. I felt a tugging within me. I listened intently for a baby's cry but heard nothing except the perinatologist and surgery techs speaking intently to one another.

Seemingly without warning, the perinatologist held up a reddish, wet baby—our first baby boy! Matthew had arrived! The NICU team whisked him to their station and began oxygen as they vigorously rubbed, weighed, and measured him. I watched as they placed him on the scale: 4 lbs. 7 ounces, it read. As I watched the nurses work with Matthew, a second baby joined him. Luke was here! He was pink, wet, and wiggly, with dark hair. I watched as the nurses placed him on the scale: 4 lbs. 14 ounces. Luke was under an oxygen hood, and a nurse held a mask near Matthew. I watched intently as the NICU team swaddled the boys tightly. They brought them over to where I still lay on the surgery table. They pressed one, then the other against my cheek, and whisked them off. Matthew went straight to the NICU, and Luke went to the regular nursery.

Someone wheeled me into recovery, where I dozed in a darkened room while a nurse typed away on her computer and periodically checked on me. After an hour, the nurse wheeled me past the regular nursery to my room. Mark stood in the nursery near Luke's bassinet. Mark came around and talked to us. The doctors planned to move Luke to the NICU as well.

The nurse wheeled me to my new hospital room, settled me in, and ordered a food service tray. My parents left to go home since I was settled and the boys were safely in the NICU. Mark wheeled me down to the NICU to see the boys. We donned paper gowns and went to meet our baby boys. Matthew lay on an incubator table under a light, an oxygen hood resting over his head. Tubes and wires trailed from his tiny veins, and a feeding tube was in his nose. His name was taped to his incubator and decorated with Halloween stickers. The nurse removed his oxygen hood for a moment so I could touch him. His head was smaller than the palm of my hand; he had wispy brown hair. A preemie diaper swallowed him, and his beanie drooped over his eyes.

Luke lay in an incubator beside Matthew, with a similar name tag and Halloween stickers. He, too, was enveloped by a preemie diaper and beanie. Luke was pink and healthy-looking with rosebud lips and dark hair. Like Matthew, tubes and wires snaked across his incubator from his tiny veins; he, too, had a feeding tube. I couldn't hold Luke either, but I could touch him. His head was larger than Matthew's but still fit in the palm of my hand.

Mark wheeled me back to my room, said his goodbyes, and left for home. I was concerned for the boys, but they were in capable hands in the NICU. There was nothing I could do, so I began to pray. I prayed over them, committing them to God's powerful yet tender care. I prayed for Mark and myself as we started this daunting journey. Somewhere along the way, the pain medication overtook me, and I drifted off to sleep.

My mother was there early the following day, and I was given clearance to walk down to the NICU. I could also hold Matthew and Luke and was encouraged to try to nurse them. Luke caught on quickly but grew frustrated by the scarcity of my milk production. Matthew struggled with the process and grew tired quickly.

Mark arrived and relayed his plans to drive his parents down to the hospital later that afternoon so they could meet the boys. Later that afternoon, they all came, nervous about meeting their grandsons. We all gowned up and went in to see the boys. At first, Mark's folks seemed overwhelmed by their tubes and wires and how tiny the boys were; however, Mark's mother warmed to the idea of holding Luke first and then Matthew.

Her eyes glistened as she blinked away tears. She held Luke, looked up at Mark, and said, "Look at you, Mark. All grown up and married with babies."

I stayed in the hospital another day. Nurses encouraged me to pump breast milk for Luke, as he quickly devoured what little I could send. Nurses encouraged me to continue to pump to stimulate production, but very little happened. After my release, I still had to return to the NICU daily to try to nurse the boys. My mom came to care for me as I recovered from surgery. Since I wasn't cleared to drive, she drove me to the hospital every day to nurse the boys and be with them. When my mom could not come, church friends drove me daily, and Mark drove down after work to get me.

Within ten days, Luke was released from the NICU. Upon Luke's release, we were expected to stay overnight at the hospital in a special room for parents taking home preemies —a trial run, so to speak, with caring for him overnight. We spent a fitful night in the hospital, rising at two-hour intervals. I would first try to nurse him, supplement him with formula, put him back to sleep, and repeat the process in two hours.

By morning, Mark and I were exhausted, but we had passed the new parent test with Luke and were released. We packed Luke into the baby carrier with his apnea and heart monitor and began the drive home. The car's motion agitated him; he started screaming and continued screaming most of the way home. Mark snaked through the busy traffic as I sat in the back with Luke, trying to console him. Once home, we lugged Luke inside, and all his monitors, diaper bag, and hospital papers, and plopped down, frazzled and exhausted. Our lives had just changed.

Our life quickly became an exhausting cycle of feeding Luke every two hours while I tried my best to pump enough breast milk to take to the hospital for Matthew. After two weeks in the NICU, Matthew came home. My mother drove up almost daily to help me settle into a routine with the boys. Mark took a week off work to do the same. We settled into our labor-intensive routine of feeding Matthew every two hours and Luke every three hours. I continued my exhausting and futile attempts at pumping. Mark's mother came to stay, helping us immensely. She slept in the spare bedroom and got up each night with me as I nursed and bottle-fed the boys. She worked beside me all day, helping me feed and diaper the boys and helping me tackle our newly acquired mountain of laundry. After a week, she went home, and I was on my own.

In the wee hours, two thoughts ran consistently through my mind: the family of which I'd dreamed long ago had taken shape, and I was in awe of what God had done. I prayed for His protection and providential care over our remaining embryo babies in cryopreservation. The second thought was an acknowledgment of the massive responsibility now laid upon me as a mother to preemie twins.

In a far-away corner of my mind, the sun-drenched farmgirl in her orange sundress stood silent and still, lifting the seedlings of those carefully nurtured dreams to her Heavenly Father. She stood silent in awe of the massive work God had done. She stood still beneath two stunning realities: the reality of the daunting task ahead and the greater reality of God's ability to do marvelous things. In silence and stillness, she lifted her seedlings in hopeful expectation and refused to let them die.

CHAPTER 2

MY OWN UNDERSTANDING; HEAD-ON COLLISION WITH REALITY

"Trust in the Lord with all your heart, and do not lean on your own understanding. In all your ways acknowledge him, and he will make straight your paths."

Proverbs 3:5–6, ESV

"Your word is a lamp to my feet and a light to my path."

Psalm 119:105, ESV

It was my first week alone with my preemie twins. Mark had returned to his third shift job. His mother had come for a week and returned home. My mother had stopped coming daily, and I was on my own to care for my preemie twins, Matthew and Luke. Doctors continued to recommend feeding Matthew at two-hour intervals and Luke at three-hour intervals, as Matthew's weight gain lagged, and Luke also needed the nutrition to prompt weight gain. I remained hopeful that my pumping would prove fruitful, one day my breast milk would magically come in, and I'd be able to produce enough to feed both boys. In dutiful hope, I kept pumping every two hours. The only thing that happened was exhaustion, frustration, and less than two ounces of breast milk each time I pumped. There was no such thing as a night's sleep; my days and nights ran together in an endless stream. I fed Matthew every two hours and Luke every three hours and then caught a nap before repeating the process for the next twenty-four-hour cycle. This continued for weeks.

Since the boys were born, I noticed a marked difference in the boys' development. Luke was small, but his color was rosy and healthy-looking. He was tiny but strong, with a hearty appetite and a robust set of lungs. From the beginning, Matthew's color seemed slightly yellowish. There was no roll at the top of his ears—they looked like elf ears. Matthew also had no bridge to his nose, and across the palm of his tiny hands, there was a single line, as opposed to two or three. The doctors called it a Simian crease; it could be an indicator of long-term disability, or it could mean nothing at all. We would have to wait and see how his development progressed. The doctors also assured me his ears and nose would continue to form as he grew. The doctors were aware that Matthew struggled from the beginning more than Luke, but remained cautiously optimistic, adopting a "wait and see" attitude towards his development. They said he was still a preemie and could still make astounding gains. The opposite was also true; he could have severe developmental disabilities that could cause significant issues for him and our family. We would have to wait and see.

Our first winter was unusually cold and snowy, even by our Midwestern standards. Being preemies, the boys needed extra help to stay warm, so I moved the bassinets into the living room and kept a fire burning in the fireplace. That kept the living room ten to fifteen degrees warmer than the rest of the house. Matthew and Luke each slept in their bassinet near the fireplace. Luke slept like a little cherub, waking in time for each feeding. If I was late getting his bottle, he wailed loudly, red-faced, his tiny fists pummeling the air. Matthew slept and would have continued to sleep until he perished of hunger, so I woke him for each feeding. He would often tire during the process and drift back to sleep. I continued waking him, struggling to get the recommended three ounces per feeding down. Every feeding was a struggle.

The day arrived for the boys' first follow-up appointment since their release from the NICU. I dressed them in their matching preemie sleepers I'd received as a baby shower gift, gathered their heart and apnea monitors, bundled them against the winter cold, and loaded them in their infant carriers. Mark helped me load them and their gear into the car, and I was off to my first doctor's visit with the boys. The doctor was pleased with Luke's weight gain and development to the point that Luke no longer needed the heart and apnea monitors. He still recommended feeding Luke every three hours because he was a preemie. The doctor was both guardedly optimistic and concerned for Matthew's development. He recommended maintaining his feeding at two-hour intervals as his weight gain lagged. I mentioned how Matthew often spit up and described the grainy, dark texture at times. On cue, it seemed, Matthew spewed watery curdled glop all over the doctor —liberally speckled with reddish black grains. The doctor was unperturbed as the nurse and I hurried to mop up the foul-smelling goop. However, the doctor had ample opportunity to diagnose Matthew's condition as acid reflux and prescribed medication to alleviate the irritation. Hopefully, the medication would improve his ability to eat and gain weight. I loaded up the boys again and headed home, relieved to be rid of one set of heart and apnea monitors. Once I was at home again, the nonstop cycle of feeding and diapering the boys continued unabated. In frustration and defeat, I gave up on pumping.

Mark left for work at 11 PM and returned each morning around 7:30 AM. We passed briefly in the kitchen, exchanging a few words as he ate his breakfast and went to bed. I did my best to keep the boys as quiet as possible so he could get the rest he needed. Matthew just slept; Luke wailed loudly and inconsolably if I wasn't right on time with his bottle. It was imperative to keep Luke well-fed and quiet so Mark could sleep. Matthew had to be awakened for each feeding and kept awake long enough to eat the recommended three ounces per feeding. Since he tended to spit up most of what he ate each feeding, I did my best to keep him propped in his bouncy seat following each feeding to help deter the spitting up and keep him as awake as possible until his next feeding.

My days were spent in non-stop feedings. Unwashed dishes piled in my sink, and the baskets of laundry mounted as I struggled through the exhaustion to keep Luke fed and quiet, and Matthew alive and making progress. My body and mind slumped beneath the weight of fatigue and stress as my soul wrestled through the many inherent questions embedded within this drastic change in my life circumstances, the boys' differing development, and the faith questions that ran across the grain of what I was experiencing day to day.

I considered myself a strong, Christian woman and was committed to being an all-star wife and mother. As a mother, I dreamed of being an all-out warrior for truth and righteousness, teaching and training my thriving, God-centered family. I listened attentively to ministry programming on our Christian radio station for years and continued that practice. I couldn't wait to throw myself headlong into those pursuits as a new mother of my tiny boys. I was full of hope and expectations for how God would act on our behalf. Though I could see Matthew's needs, I was also firmly convinced of the power of prayer. I was certain that if I threw myself into faithful, fervent prayer for Matthew's needs, God would come through with flying colors. Matthew would catch up to Luke in no time, and all his early delays would become a distant memory. All I had to do was pray faithfully and fervently, and God would grant my requests by delivering my version of a wonderful Christian life. With all this in mind, I set my heart on praying intently and at great length so God would see how fervently I desired this life for His honor and glory. I began the practice of singing hymns, praying over my tiny boys, and committing them to God's tender care.

As I softly sang, *"Great is thy faithfulness, O God my Father, There is no shadow of turning with Thee . . ."* I reminded myself that my Lord never changed. His faithfulness in giving me these boys was the same faithfulness that would sustain me now. As I sang, *"Strength for today and bright hope for tomorrow. . ."* I claimed His sustaining grace for that day, that hour, and whatever days lay ahead.

The realities of life with preemie twins were hitting hard and fast. My days continued with the rigorous feeding schedule, responding to Matthew's beeping heart and apnea monitors, and diapering the boys. Matthew's feeding issues were present from the beginning and continued even with the medication his doctor prescribed. His sucking reflex was weak and underdeveloped, and he tired quickly. My nights were the same as my days. My workload was exhausting, thankless, and nonstop. I saw no one besides Mark and the boys for weeks. Since I was a young girl, I'd dreamed of being a stay-at-home mom. This was not what I envisioned; life was not turning out as I expected.

Along with the exhausting and stunningly difficult caregiving routines that had become my life, another struggle brewed beneath the surface. Because the expectations that lived in my head and the realities in my house were worlds apart, it wasn't long before I faced a brutal clash between those lofty expectations and life on the ground. Life was not playing out as I wanted or as I expected. God was not doing what I thought He ought to do. He was not healing Matthew as I asked. I was doing everything humanly possible to be a great mom, good Christian, and stellar wife. He was not making life easier for me. I was operating at levels of exhaustion I never knew existed. I was scrambling to snatch a moment for quiet time. I was neither knocking it out of the proverbial park nor looking good doing it. I was shocked and stunned by the workload, constancy, and thankless nature.

I said things to myself like: "So, this is now my life for the next 18 years? What have I done?" I questioned whether we had run ahead of God's plan by pursuing IVF and whether Matthew's delays were the result. My mind thrashed about in confusion. Had I misunderstood Him, His Word, and His plan? Was I on the right path spiritually at all? I was confident this was the right path early on, but now I wasn't sure. It certainly looked and felt very different than I expected. There was nothing to do but forge ahead and learn how, not only to survive, but thrive under the heavy load of Matthew's obvious needs and care-giving around the clock.

I lay, bloodied, in the wreckage of deep disappointment. I prayed fervently, yet God was not answering as I thought He should. Matthew made little progress. Mark remained on the graveyard shift. My house was a wreck; laundry, dishes, and the boys' needs were constant. I had little interaction with anyone outside the home. My plans for stellar early morning quiet times ran aground upon my exhaustion. Brutal self-condemnation badgered and belittled me. I knew I was in a battle that I was perpetually losing. My only resource, it seemed, was crying out to God as I slumped to the ground day after day in exhaustion and defeat. What saved me from sinking into the abyss of despair was the truth I'd learned years ago at our farmhouse breakfast table, underscored by the truth pouring into my kitchen through our local Christian radio station.

By Christmas, Luke was eating heartily and making progress with ease. Matthew still struggled to suck, swallow, and keep down what little he ate. He gained weight at a snail's pace and struggled to hold up his head. The doctors continued to express concern for Matthew but still assured me in their next breath that these struggling preemies often make astounding gains with little lasting effects. I clung to those words in hope, firmly placing my faith in God to do His extraordinary work as I prayed. At the same time, I could see Matthew's lagging development. During our frequent attempts at tummy time, Matthew would lie face down with his face smashed into the blanket. He could quickly smother if left unattended. He could not hold up his head. Despite my coaxing and support, his progress was minuscule.

As the new year rolled in, both boys got sick with an intestinal virus. Luke had a few miserable days but rebounded nicely and was largely unphased. Matthew did not. Since he already struggled to eat and maintain his weight, the onset of his intestinal symptoms caused severe weight loss within days. I called the nurse line at our primary doctor's office. The nurses said to let the virus run its course and assured me he would be better within a few days. I was unsure. At the pace Matthew was both dropping weight and weakening, I feared he might be in a terrible place if his symptoms didn't improve quickly. I continued to coax him to eat. One afternoon, his alertness and his color began changing rapidly. I called the doctor's office and made an appointment; they had a cancellation within less than an hour.

I woke Mark so he could stay with Luke, packed up Matthew, and took him to the doctor's appointment. I sat bedraggled in the small, crowded waiting room with Matthew's diaper bag stuffed behind me in the chair as I held him in his infant carrier in my lap. A little girl with wildly curling dark hair and a runny nose stood at my elbow, peering into the infant carrier. She looked from Matthew's pale face to mine with a questioning gaze. "Yes, he's sick, Honey. That's why we're here to see the doctor. She will help him feel better," I said. The girl nodded but seemed unconvinced. I wasn't convinced either, but I smiled at her reassuringly. Matthew squirmed and began to cry in his carrier. I gave him a bottle and hoped it would stay down. His stomach gurgled audibly as the nurse appeared and called my wild-haired companion back to an exam room. I moved Matthew's infant carrier to the neighboring chair, continued to work to feed him, and waited. More nurses appeared, calling more children and parents into exam rooms; the waiting room was clearing. Soon, Matthew and I were alone in the waiting room. The receptionist peered over the counter at us.

"What time is your appointment?" she asked. "The doctor is swamped," she said. "She'll be with you shortly." She smiled reassuringly. Matthew's stomach gurgled loudly again, and he began squirming and crying. Almost immediately, a nurse appeared and took us to an exam room. She had me undress him so she could weigh him; he'd dropped nearly two pounds. She cast me a questioning glance; I nodded, agreeing with her concern. She finished her preliminary exam, plopped Matthew's chart into the rack outside the door, and left, leaving the door ajar. Our doctor stood at the counter outside our exam room charting. She caught my eye, indicating she would be with us soon. Matthew began crying and squirming once again. His stomach audibly gurgled once again as his bowels erupted in a massive blow-out. His tiny diaper was soaked and dripping. The paper topping the exam table became a foul-smelling pool. I lifted Matthew off the soggy paper, folding the edges to prevent it from dripping onto the floor.

"I need help!" I called over my shoulder. Our nurse appeared, gasping audibly. She sprang into action, swiping away the soggy paper into a special trash bag, spraying down the table, and rolling out fresh paper. She was helping me change and clean up Matthew when the doctor arrived, gazing curiously at the commotion. The nurse briefly explained. The doctor looked aghast at the front of my sweatshirt; it was heavily smeared with foul-smelling goo. I took it off, glad it hadn't soaked my tee shirt. I tossed my soiled sweatshirt into the special trash bag along with the soiled diaper and paper. Without warning, Matthew began squirming and crying once again; his bowels exploded again in another significant blowout! The doctor and nurse gaped; the nurse sprang into action again as the doctor looked over Matthew's chart. She asked the doctor if his weight was correct. She nodded; the doctor wanted to re-do it and see for herself. The nurse obliged; it was accurate. The doctor noted his weakness and poor color; she stood quietly shaking her head, the wheels in her mind turning.

"Little mister Matthew, poor guy," she said. She turned to me, "He needs intervention. He needs to be where he can get fluids and get this virus under control. He needs to be in the hospital. I'll call the transport team, and we'll get him some help," she said. "What do you need, Mom?" she asked.

I was stunned but relieved. My hunch was correct; Matthew was in danger and needed immediate help. He would receive the intervention he needed at the hospital. I had no idea what I needed, except I knew I must stay near Matthew. I called Mark and told him Matthew was being transported to the hospital and that I was going with him when the transport team arrived. My van would still be in the parking lot at the doctor's office. Mark would need to figure out those logistics with the help of a church friend. The news rattled him, but he was glad Matthew would receive the help he needed.

The transport team arrived; they were a professional and fit-looking team tightly zipped into navy blue jumpsuits. They strapped Matthew onto the gurney; he looked smaller and even more pathetic on the small gurney. I grabbed my purse and Matthew's diaper bag and followed the transport team onto the waiting ambulance. The trip downtown was a blur; I numbly followed the transport team through the maze of hallways and elevators as they deposited Matthew in a hospital room and transferred him into the care of the nurses. The nurses gathered around him, taking vitals and asking me questions. I did my best to answer, relaying my concerns about his intestinal virus and drastic weight loss. They assured me he was in good hands and urged me to sit down, pointing to the teal vinyl recliner in the hospital room. I sat, nervously scanning the hospital room, still holding my purse and Matthew's diaper bag.

Lab techs were on their way, the nurses said. They would draw blood for lab work; the nurses would test his stool for rotavirus. The lab techs came and went as I sat staring, still holding my purse and Matthew's diaper bag. The nurses asked if I needed anything; I couldn't think enough to answer them, so I shook my head. My phone buzzed; it was Mark seeking an update. I told him what I knew: Matthew's room number and lab techs were drawing lab work and taking stool samples for possible rotavirus. I had no idea of anything beyond that. He mentioned coming down and bringing me a change of clothes; a church friend would stay with Luke. I agreed, and he hung up. I set down my purse and Matthew's diaper bag and stood near Matthew's bedside. My mind flashed back to his NICU days when he was nearly covered in tubes, tape, and tiny wires; I was used to seeing him this way, but this time was different. He was so weak, pale, and sickly, but he was in the right place. My relief was coupled with a deep, quiet sadness. A thought rose and bounced about my head, refusing to settle: this would be the first of many hospital stays for Matthew. This was the beginning of a long journey. I knew it, but couldn't allow myself to say it out loud. To speak it made it more true in some strange way, and I couldn't fully believe it yet.

Mark arrived with a change of clothes, a few granola bars, and water bottles. He'd taken the night off work, and our church friend agreed to stay with Luke; Mark had put Luke to bed and was prepared to stay with me at the hospital that night. The nurse brought linens and showed us how to transform the sofa into a bed. We spent a fitful night together in the hospital and woke early, waiting for an update from the doctor. The doctor confirmed rotavirus and said Matthew should stay in the hospital for several more days. Mark went home, relieving our church friend from Luke's care, and I resumed my post: waiting in a hospital room for whatever came next during our stay. With IV fluids, Matthew started to perk up. He became more alert and wakeful and began taking a bottle once again. The doctors started talking about sending him home. I was relieved, thankful, and saddened. I was relieved that he was gaining strength and thankful that he was turning a corner and headed in the right direction. I was saddened because, though I couldn't say it yet, I knew we would be back.

Once we were home, the same exhausting routine kicked into overdrive once again. The disparity between the boys' development was becoming increasingly apparent. While Luke jumped and played vigorously in his bouncer, I wrapped Matthew in receiving blankets to support him in his bouncer, and I rolled receiving blankets into a collar to support his head. There he would be, wedged and propped in an upright position to keep down what little he ate and to provide a different position other than lying down or being carried. While Luke giggled, squawked, and sputtered, Matthew simply hung there. I expressed my concern to our primary doctors during a regular visit. I was relieved yet unsettled when she recommended physical therapy at our local children's hospital. The same unsettled thought that began bouncing about my head during Matthew's rotavirus hospitalization rose to stare me down with a knowing gaze. The start of Matthew's physical therapy meant I packed up the boys bi-weekly for our trips to the children's hospital downtown. Matthew would often be worn out from travel time, the trek through the hospital, and wait time. He was either hungry, getting sleepy, or sound asleep during his therapy sessions; most sessions proved futile.

Life was not working out as I planned. Matthew's development lagged no matter how fervently I prayed. My workload continued relentlessly. My isolation and exhaustion concerned no one, it seemed. I was doing all I knew to do to be a godly wife and mother. I was doing all I knew to do to get God's attention through my ongoing prayers. I was working from the solid foundation laid down by God-honoring parents and from premises I believed marked the life of stellar saints. I believed that life as a truly godly person was marked by flawless performance in spiritual disciplines. My prayers should rock the heavens with spot-on precision and fervency. I believed God would honor those fervent, on-point prayers with the answers I sought, delivering my version of the wonderful Christian life. I was quickly discovering, in very real and raw ways, that it was untrue. Scripture was true; Christ was the way, the truth, and the life, as He'd always been. However, the belief system I had crafted was faulty and flimsy. It would not support me in these difficult times, which would mark my life for the foreseeable future.

I was raised in the church and knew that Scripture and prayer were supposed to hold the key to all the power and insight I would ever need. The spiritual disciplines all good Christians should master were taught and modeled early in my life. At this point in my life, these disciplines had been tested only in the trials that marked high school, college, and young adulthood. Now, two tiny humans were dependent upon me for their survival. My faith was solid but untested. My understanding of prayer, Scripture, surrender, and faith was firm and on point but mostly exercised as discussion topics in ladies' Bible studies and Sunday School classes. No deep hardship had descended upon me that forced my faith from the realm of knowledge and theory into action. Now, both my survival and my boys' survival were dependent upon the power and strength of my faith in God.

The realities that descended upon me as a new mom forced my faith into action. On one hand, the possibility of descending into the abyss of depression and despair loomed large. To succumb meant I could become incapacitated and unable to care for the boys as they needed. On the other hand, I could learn to put my faith into action and learn the skills I needed to, not merely survive, but thrive in this difficult place. I had no other recourse. If prayer was everything Scripture claimed, it was powerful, and I needed to learn to use it. If Scripture truly contained all truth, wisdom, and insight, and was a deep source of strength that it claimed to be, I needed to absorb every word of it because I was in desperate need. If the Holy Spirit was truly the link to our divine power source, I needed to be plugged in every moment of the day. I soon realized

I was in over my head and there was no way out—but straight up and straight down. Straight up, by looking to Him for strength, wisdom, and power, and straight down on my knees in prayer.

I knew true faith was the answer. I knew Scripture was the key to the treasure trove of what I needed. However, I was forced to deconstruct the myths I'd adopted. Working off the solid foundation already laid by godly parents, I had to rebuild an impenetrable faith fortress based upon the truth of Scripture. The task at hand was to dig into Scripture and mine out the truths that would be the bricks and mortar of my faith fortress. I also must act upon those same truths I mined out of scripture. In so doing, layer the bricks of truth with the mortar of faithful obedience to build this faith fortress in His strength.

In faithful obedience, I began digging to unearth what God truly promises His followers, what He wants for us, and how authentic prayer looks and sounds. I wondered how I came to the idea that God desired to fulfill my dreams and give me an easy life. In scripture, I found that He promised hardship rather than ease. At every turn, though, He promised His presence, His peace, and the assurance that there is a deeper purpose behind our current suffering. Also, the common theme emerged that He is doing something deeper, larger, and more profound than we can imagine. Despite our current angst, our struggle is not lost on Him, nor is it for nothing. However, I also found very little was said about God changing circumstances in my favor. I found little about God providing a life of comfort and ease. As I continued to search the scriptures, it became apparent that He desires to engage humans in a life-changing relationship. He accepts us the way He finds us but has no intention of allowing us to remain there. He desires to confront us with truth, change us, and draw us to Himself in ongoing and ever-increasing intimacy. The Ancient of Days desired to engage *me*, change *me*, and draw *me* into intimate friendship with Himself—it astounded me. How could I refuse?

It became increasingly clear that this life of faith was less about perfect performance or meeting the high benchmarks I set for myself. It was about listening to Him, doing what He asked, and following in trust and faith. It was less about learning interesting facts about Him in Scripture and more about learning Him, His voice, His ways, and His heart through immersion in His Word.

I knew the Psalms held a treasure trove of authentic and raw prayers that genuinely expressed the writers' heart cry to God, so I began marinating my soul in them. I found that the psalmist often ranted, complained, vented in anger, and lamented in raw, unvarnished ways. I identified and took up many psalms as my heart's cry. The unedited emotion permitted me to pray in the same way. Along the way, my prayers changed. They shifted from attempts to lobby Him for fulfillment of my tightly held dreams into a state of surrender. I learned to stop tearfully pounding His chest, trying to convince Him that my way was better. Frankly, I became too exhausted to fight Him any longer and began to sink into His everlasting arms, sob on His chest, and learn of Him. My dependence upon Him became a matter of sanity and survival. I had little contact outside the home, and Matthew's needs were intense.

The Scriptures I read melded with the sermons I listened to on Christian radio. One sermon series in particular by Chuck Swindoll shaped how I viewed my life situation from that point forward. It was a biographical series on Moses, and he focused on Moses's forty years in Midian. Seasons of prolonged hardship, he declared, were special seasons that build grit and character unlike any other. It's where we learn to serve faithfully in obscurity with no thought of escaping or fast-forwarding through it all. We simply submit to the place and station where He has placed us, learn the lessons only that place can teach us, and trust God to move us out of that place if, or when, He chooses.

The proverbial lightbulb switched on over my head. I was living in Midian. This isolated place of endless, thankless work, coupled with the realities of Matthew's needs, was my Midian—and I began to refer to my Midian-like situation as "the barren place." If God thought enough of me to stick me in "the barren place," who was I to balk or complain? In this crucible, His intent was purification, not cruelty. I was humbled that He deemed me worth the time and attention of purification. Perhaps He saw something priceless, some glittering gem, now in raw form, that was worth His effort to unearth. In this crucible of "the barren place," perhaps it would become a glowing monument of His grace.

In "the barren place," my task was to submit to the lessons only learned in this place of menial service. I was to serve faithfully for my audience of One and trust His timing and sovereign hand through it all. He had placed me in this "barren place" on purpose. He knew I was a Midian-dweller before I knew it. It became clear that unbeknownst to me, the faith fortress I'd been building had been in the "barren place" all this time. He knew I would need a strong faith-fortress before I knew it and set me to work on its construction. I had to persevere in that undertaking. After all, Moses dwelt in Midian for forty years. This became a guiding mindset of my life from that point forward. Like Moses' stay in Midian, my sojourn in "the barren place" could be lengthy as well.

My mother, who is also an RN, came often to see the boys and me in the first year, and I valued her skill and practical help. During one of those visits, we sat at the kitchen table finishing our lunch. Matthew was wedged and propped up in his bouncer beside me. Mom's gaze continually fell upon him, brows furrowed, yet saying little. She called me later, relaying her grave concerns about Matthew's delays, suggesting cerebral palsy as chief among them. She pondered that more factors accounted for his delays than just his status as a preemie. Following that conversation with Mom, the stunning possibility descended that Matthew may have long-standing health and developmental issues that may be within God's perfect plan for him and our family. Matthew would likely never catch up to Luke developmentally. Until that conversation, I had never considered a long-term, irreversible condition like a genetic syndrome or long-term developmental disability as Matthew's reality—or ours.

However, as this journey played out, it was becoming increasingly apparent that these two realities could coexist—a special needs child *and* God's perfect plan. The road before me would likely be very different from what I planned. God's plan wasn't always up and to the right, but it is always good. I'd read and heard stories of great hardship, but never dreamt ours could be among them.

The realities of a child with special needs loomed large and daunting. This was neither the life I dreamed of nor wanted. My battle with deep disappointment raged on. What I hoped would happen if I prayed hard enough would likely never happen, no matter how fervently I prayed. For some inexplicable reason, God was saying "no" to my honest and heartfelt requests for Matthew's healing. I'd heard so many stories of healing and restoration throughout my life and hoped ours could be among them. As our story unfolded, it became increasingly clear that it would not happen.

Our primary doctors set the wheels in motion for a consultation with a pediatrician specializing in developmental disabilities. With mom's concerns of cerebral palsy clanging in my head, Mark, Matthew, and I went to the appointment while my mother stayed with Luke. We were ushered into a large windowed room. The pediatrician and a team of medical students filed in. The doctor seated himself in front of us, and the medical students arranged themselves in a half-circle behind him—lab coats crisp and white, clipboards clutched, sharp pencils poised. The doctor asked a barrage of questions and listened to our concerns. I struggled to listen to the doctor, handle Matthew, and ask intelligent questions. Frankly, the appointment was a blur of questions without answers and heavy realities settling firmly upon me. The pediatrician had seen many cases like Matthew's, as his expertise was developmental disabilities. Developmental disabilities were indeed Matthew's reality and ours. They were not going to correct themselves, and it was becoming starkly apparent they would mark our lives in significant ways.

The appointment set in motion a series of screenings and tests to rule out hearing and vision issues, genetic syndromes, and a myriad of other possibilities. One blessing was that it also set the wheels in motion for in-home therapy through First Steps, which eliminated our bi-weekly treks downtown. It also meant I would have a steady stream of therapists in my home until Matthew turned three and was aged out of the program. I had become familiar with special needs over time, but after that consultation, I was suddenly plunged into that world. Medical, educational, and therapy lingo were all foreign languages I would have to learn quickly to advocate for Matthew. Well-meaning people bombarded me with books and articles and directed me to websites touting holistic cure-alls and nutritional remedies, pressing me to try them. My days were spent in the same demanding caregiving routine, with the weighty realities of Matthew's needs settling upon me at every turn. The initial round of tests came back indicating Matthew did not have cerebral palsy, vision, or hearing issues, nor a genetic syndrome. There was relief in many ways, yet it presented more unanswered questions.

I knew God could be trusted; I knew His ways were best.

I knew He was doing something deep and wonderful, but this seemed like the wrong route to that destination. If I truly believed all I claimed to, there was no other option but total surrender of the dream that Matthew would be healed. If God chose to heal him, that was His business. My business was following Him. If He asked me to release something even so precious as Matthew's healing, He knew what He was doing. Though I didn't understand His ways, I trusted His heart and knew He would carry us through the journey ahead, however that looked.

My disappointment, however, was deep and ever-present. To each honest and heartfelt request, I listened to one "no" after another. Healing for my infant son seemed like a reasonable request. A large, godly family seemed like an honorable request. A truth-centered writing and teaching ministry seemed well-intentioned and pure. However, if I claimed to be a Christ-follower, my only option was to release each cherished dream at His request. Sad and broken, I watched helplessly as each precious dream slipped silently away. However, I also knew that something given over to God is never truly lost. Anything precious He asks us to release to Him He holds for safekeeping. In His wisdom, He will give back to us those precious things entrusted to His care—in ways we least expect and in ways that are good for us and bring Him glory. I had to believe that even my tightly held and carefully guarded girlhood dream could be entrusted to His care. He would keep it safe and protected if I just released it into His tender care. In a corner of my mind, that sun-kissed farmgirl in her orange sundress collapsed in sad yet trusting surrender. Open-handed, she released it all—the large brood of boys, the long farmhouse table—to her Heavenly Father.

Luke learned to pull up and crawl with ease and began attempting a few tentative steps at ten months old; in no time, it seemed, he was not only walking but running. As he learned his first words, when he said Matthew's name, it came out as "Matt-new", and the moniker stuck. As Luke progressed, he also began to notice a difference in Matthew.

One afternoon, I had laid the boys in their respective cribs for naps. As I began tackling the mound of dishes in the kitchen sink, I heard a small voice from the boys' room. I tiptoed down the hallway and peered into their room where their cribs stood in an "L" shape to fit them into their small room. Luke was standing in his crib, peering into Matthew's crib and calling to him: "Hi! Hi! Hi!"Luke called, trying to elicit a response from Matthew. Matthew just laid in his crib, mouthing his hands. Undaunted, Luke shimmied and writhed over the end of his crib and tumbled into Matthews'. I watched as Luke snuggled beside Matthew. "Hi! Hi, Matt-new! Hi, Matt-new!" he kept saying.

I slipped quietly into the room; Luke glanced up at me, the thousand questions he longed to formulate rose to meet my gaze. "I know, Buddy. He doesn't say 'Hi!' back, does he?" I said, "He wants to, but doesn't know how yet; maybe he will learn,". Matthew finally smiled impishly and nestled against Luke. "Look Buddy," I said, "Matthew is smiling. He likes you snuggling by him and talking to him.". A sad, quiet knowing settled in my chest; Luke would have a brother, a twin brother, in fact, that he would only know in a limited way. Matthew's needs would affect our entire family-each of us differently, yet profoundly. Despite the disparity in their development, Luke continued his attempts to engage Matthew. When Matthew was a year old, he learned to roll over, and it wasn't uncommon for Matthew to roll himself into corners or under chairs until he was stuck. In an attempt to engage Matthew, Luke often got on the floor with him, and the two of them rolled about the living room floor. When Matthew got stuck, Luke would come and tell me, "Matt-new's stuck!". As Matthew neared two years old, he was pulling up and walking around furniture. Our First Steps therapists suggested finding an older-style walker that would allow Matthew to practice walking while gaining skill and confidence. We found one, and soon Matthew was following Luke everywhere in his walker. Luke enjoyed it, and it wasn't uncommon for Luke to help Matthew drink from his sippy cup or feed Matthew crackers or animal cookies as they hung out together. Luke kept talking to him, snuggling him, and saying, "I 'wuv' you, Matt-new!". Matthew just smiled impishly, snuggled Luke in return as best as he could, and said nothing.

Church friends put us in touch with a lady in our congregation who was also an occupational therapist and who had hands-on experience dealing with special needs children. She came simply to help us bear the burden of Matthew's obvious needs and provide whatever assistance she could. Teresa became a special friend to Matthew and our family. As soon as she witnessed Matthew's incessant hand-flapping, mouthing his hands and objects, and his kicking, she immediately recognized his sensory-seeking behaviors and began helping and supporting me as I tried to handle Matthew's needs.

The descending reality of life with a special needs child was the beginning of a long grieving process. With each milestone Luke crossed with ease and exuberance lay the gnawing reality that Matthew had not, and likely would not, cross it as well. Uncovering Luke's delightful personality and his early fascination with the natural world, books, and great musical works was bittersweet. Matthew's personality remained shrouded in his medical and developmental issues, discovered only by those undaunted by his needs. I never wanted to be the mother of a special needs child, but I was one. I didn't like it, but I loved Matthew and was filled with compassion for him.

My only comfort was found in Scripture. I read and re-read the stories of Job, Joseph, Moses, Esther, and Ruth. The big reward for their hardships, it seemed, was an intimate friendship with God. If that was the route planned for me—to transform me into a Moses or an Esther—how could I refuse? To be among the strong, courageous, and honored saints required hardship, that was obvious. It seemed like He pointed me toward the two sons within my care and the mundane tasks of mothering, instructing me to learn Him there.

FOOD FOR THOUGHT:

1. When have your expectations slammed head-on into life's realities? What was the result? How did Scripture help you make sense of your situation? How can Scripture help us lay out truth-based expectations? What does He truly promise?

2. When have you suffered a major disappointment? How did it affect you? How did you handle it? How did Scripture help?

CHAPTER 3

KNOWING WHO LEADS ME– EVEN UP THE STEEP PATH

". . .fear not, for I am with you; be not dismayed, for I am your God; I will strengthen you, I will help you, I will uphold you with my righteous right hand."

Isaiah 41:10, ESV

"Blessed is the man who trusts in the Lord, whose trust is in the Lord. He is like a tree planted by water, that sends out its roots by the stream, and does not fear when heat comes, for its leaves remain green, and is not anxious in the year of drought, for it does not cease to bear fruit."

Jeremiah 17:7-8, ESV

Would you entrust your life to someone you barely knew? Me either! That would be foolhardy. However, as Christians, God repeatedly urges us to entrust Him with our earthly lives and our eternity. That sounds like an impossibly big ask, especially if we aren't quite sure who He is or if He's worthy of that magnitude of trust.

I began to find that the more I immersed myself in Scripture, the more deeply acquainted with Him I became. The more I knew Him, the more I found He was more than worthy of my complete trust. Though I didn't know how our circumstances might play out, I knew the One Who was in total control. I knew He was doing something deeply significant in and through my difficult circumstances, and I found deep, settled peace in that knowledge. I found the One Who formed earth and heaven, called His people out of paganism and into relationship with Him, was the same God Who spoke with me over my kitchen sink. I found the same Yahweh Sabbaoth who humbled Egypt with plagues, parted the Red Sea, and thundered from Sinai, was the same One Who heard the inarticulate groanings of my heart. The more I learned of Him in Scripture, the more I knew He was more than able to sustain my boys and me in our overwhelming flood of circumstances.

This trust in God was severely tested as circumstances took another nosedive. The boys were eighteen months old, and it was the evening of July Fourth. Luke was playing around the house as I worked on dinner. Since Matthew lagged in his walking, our First Steps therapist suggested an older-style walker to help Matthew learn to walk. We found one, and Matthew followed Luke everywhere in that walker. Matthew's teething process was in full swing as he worked at cutting molars. It was agonizingly slow and painful for him. When teething, he drooled excessively, was congested, and was generally a drooly, snotty mess. Mark was outside mowing when I saw Matthew stiffen, his teeth clenched. His eyes rolled up into his head as his body trembled. It lasted only a moment, and then he acted normally again. It stunned me. I'd never seen anything like it. When Mark came in from mowing, I mentioned it to him, he nodded knowingly.

"It was probably a seizure," he said. He mentioned his boyhood friend who suffered from seizures. He'd witnessed them and said Matthew may have another one before the evening was over.

Mark and I had just sat down to dinner. Matthew followed Luke into the back bedroom in his walker. I went to check on them, and it happened again. I yelled for Mark; he recognized it immediately, confirming it was a seizure. We loaded the boys into our van and drove to our local emergency room. We were ushered from the waiting room into a curtained-off bay and waited. Mark told the doctor that he'd witnessed seizures before and had recognized Matthew's episode. The doctor admitted his lack of knowledge and experience with childhood seizures but admitted Matthew for overnight observation. I stayed overnight with Matthew. Mark and Luke went home.

Matthew and I were ushered into a small room with a wall of windows, and the air conditioning running full blast. An irritable nurse settled him in and pointed me toward a narrow, bench-like couch beneath the windows, indicating I could sleep there. She pointed to the hand-held buzzer, instructing me to buzz her if I needed something. She clearly did not want to be bothered by me, Matthew, or my buzzer. There was no way sleep was in my future. I located a blanket and chair in the dim light from the hallway. I covered myself against the blasting AC and pulled the chair beside his crib, resting my head against the wall. The smell of onions wafted up from my tee shirt stained with cooking splatters; I sighed deeply and let my tears run down my neck. As I prayed, I wiped them away on my oniony-smelling tee shirt.

"Lord," I prayed, "it's me again. What's happening? We're here in the hospital. Matthew had a seizure? What? Please help us. Please help poor Matthew. I don't know what's happening, and I need You now. Please show up. Please come to our rescue." In the dim light from the hallway and the wall of windows, I could see Matthew's outline as he slept under the white hospital blanket. I listened to his slow rhythmic breathing mixed with the gurgle of his congestion. I stood beside the wall of windows, gazing out at the hospital rooftop in the light of the moon and streetlights. I continued to lift wordless prayers of tears mingled with an inarticulate groaning from the deep recesses of my soul. I returned to my chair beside Matthew's bedside, leaned my head back against the wall, and just sat in the darkness watching Matthew sleep, praying, and listening for the distinct sound of another seizure. The night droned on, the sky changed from inky black to deep charcoal gray. Then I heard it—the sound I'd heard at home. I jumped up fumbling in the darkness for the buzzer; I couldn't find it. I called for the nurse. She was not happy.

"Use the buzzer! You'll wake the whole unit! What do you need?" she flipped on the overhead light and glared at me.

"He had another seizure," I said. "He made the same sound; his eyes rolled up, and he went stiff like he was at home."

She lowered the crib rail and examined him. "He's not having one now! Are you sure? How long was it? What type was it?" she questioned.

"Yes ma'am, I'm sure. It was the same as at home. I don't know how long or what type," I replied.

She shook her head, lowered the crib rail, and turned to leave. Then I heard it again, he was having another seizure. She watched him closely, examined him again, and raised the crib rail.

"Yep, that's a seizure. You need to be downtown where they can handle children with seizures. We can't handle that here. I'll call the doc," she said, still clearly annoyed. She flipped off the light and returned to the nurses' station. I resumed my waiting place beside Matthew's bedside; it was nearly 4 AM. I could text Mark with an update by 6 AM. Luke was an early riser and would have Mark up by then.

The nurse returned with an update. They were transferring us downtown to the children's hospital. The transport team was on their way. When they arrived, I should be ready to go. She thrust forward a jumble of papers on a clipboard and asked me to sign for his discharge and transfer, impatiently huffing as she highlighted the lines for my signatures. I dutifully signed. I was ready to get Matthew the help he needed and be away from the ill-tempered nurse.

The transport team arrived. It was the same fit-looking crew zipped snuggly into their navy jumpsuits. They deftly transferred Matthew to the gurney. I snatched up my purse and Matthew's diaper bag and followed them down the hall into the elevator. They punched a series of buttons on the panel, the door slid shut, and we descended. The door slid open again and we were quickly aboard the transport van. I sat at the end of Matthew's gurney with my purse over my shoulder and his diaper bag in my lap. The team assessed Matthew and asked me a series of questions as we pulled out. I called Mark from the transport vehicle and gave him the update. He was saddened and shaken. I promised to update him when we got settled at the hospital.

At the hospital, we went straight into another transport elevator. Again, a team member punched a series of buttons and we were hurtling upward. They wheeled Matthew's gurney off the elevator into an oddly familiar hallway. They wheeled him into a corner room directly across from the nurses' station. A team of smiling nurses in brightly colored scrubs received us and settled Matthew in. They said a neurologist would be in to speak with me soon. The team of nurses hovered over Matthew, taking vitals and asking me questions; as they did so, he had another seizure. The nurses administered sedating medication.

I plopped into a nearby chair away from the commotion, my purse on one shoulder and Matthew's diaper bag on the other. My eyes burned with fatigue. I grabbed my phone and dialed my mom; my early morning call jarred her. I relayed the news about Matthew's seizures; she was silent. As I relayed Matthew's room number and the hospital's location, I could hear her scratching down the information on a writing pad. She listened silently, then said, "I'm coming to the hospital. Let me get Dad off to work, then I'll be up." She assured me of her prayers for Matthew, me, and our family, and hung up. Tears stung my eyes; I blinked them away.

The nurses pointed out the couch in the corner, reminding me that it converted into a bed, and brought me linens. They kindly asked if they could get me anything, and directed me to the coffee machine in the elevator lobby. The nurses buzzed me through the double doors as I approached and I was immediately in the elevator lobby. A coffee service sat on a table. I stuck my paper cup under the spout, staring out at the hospital rooftop as the rich black coffee sputtered into my cup. The sun was coming up. Its rays sliced through the early morning fog hovering about the city. The elevator behind me opened, and a young man in a food service uniform stepped out wheeling a cart. He took a platter of pre-packaged Danish and placed them on the coffee service table. He offered me one, which I took gratefully. I returned to Matthew's room with my coffee, powdered creamer packet, and Danish. As I sipped my coffee, nibbled my Danish, and simply sat for a moment, I thought that though this road I traveled was hard, simple things like a cup of coffee, a Danish, and a moment to sit gave me a moment's reprieve. It lifted the heavy load I carried for a few moments. It gave me enough strength to carry on and I was grateful for it.

I noticed a white-haired man in a crisp white lab coat standing at the nurse's station. The nurse pointed to our room, and he approached. "Hi, I'm the neurologist on duty," he said, extending his hand. I shook his hand, and he smiled, and sat down, holding Matthew's chart. He took a deep breath, and began:

"I've been reviewing Matthew's chart and the doctor's notes. We're suggesting a protocol of tests with your consent," he said. I nodded. He named the tests; a spinal tap was among the lineup. He explained the procedures in lay terms and what data they hoped to gain from each test. He assured me that Matthew was in good hands; their neurology team was well-versed in seizure activity and Matthew was in the right place. He indicated Matthew and I would now be regular visitors to the neurology clinic. Staff would be in touch regarding scheduling once we were home. He suggested I remain in Matthew's room for the testing, as the testing procedures were upsetting for some parents. He patted my arm and smiled sadly as he left. A nurse came with a clipboard and a pen for me to sign consent forms. She kindly highlighted the lines and I signed. She said the neurology team would come to take Matthew for testing soon.

Matthew was sleeping soundly from the sedation, so I went to the elevator lobby for another cup of coffee. I returned to Matthew's room and called Mark with an update. I relayed Matthew's floor and room number. He mentioned coming down; I asked him to pack me an overnight bag with several changes of clothes and toiletries as I had no idea how long we'd be in the hospital. He said he and Luke would come down mid-afternoon.

I simply sat beside Matthew's bed and waited for the neurology team to get him for testing. As I sat, I prayed: "Lord, You've known we would be in this place all along. Please give me the strength to handle this—whatever this is. Lord, I'm so tired of being disappointed, sad and exhausted. Please give me the strength to go on."

There was a tap on the door. My mom peered in, smiling sadly. I hugged her, thanked her for coming, and asked about her trip. She wanted to know everything about Matthew's seizures, what the doctors were saying, what sort of tests they were doing, and his prognosis. She peeked into the crib at Matthew as he slept; I did my best to fill her in and get her up to speed. Then she turned and looked at me, astonished.

"You look exhausted! Have you slept? Have you eaten?" she asked.

"I haven't, but that's okay. I don't think I could eat anyway," I answered.

A nurse tapped on the door saying the neurology team was coming. She'd also overheard what I said about not eating, and brought me a food service menu indicating that patients get a meal, but Matthew would be unable to eat today so that I could order his meal for myself. She showed me how to order. She and Mom urged me to at least order something and try to eat; I would feel better, Mom said. I was unconvinced but ordered a cheeseburger.

Mom and I talked and waited. I told her everything I knew all over again. Mom urged me to walk around the unit to stay awake and move around a bit. I did so and had the same oddly familiar feeling when we entered the unit earlier that morning. As I passed the nurses' station and rounded the corner, I saw it. It was Matthew's room during his rotavirus hospitalization. I stood for a moment outside the doorway, then quickly moved on. My premonition back then had been correct. We had indeed returned. I had never considered seizures in Matthew's future back then, but it was our new reality, it seemed.

I went back to Matthew's current room and visited with Mom.

Mom pointed out the food service tray that had arrived during my walk around the unit and urged me to eat. As we were talking, a tech who had previously come to take Matthew to his spinal tap appeared at the doorway. I waved her in. The medication they had to give Matthew for complete sedation was stronger than the one they usually give, she said. Because of that, he was taking longer to wake up, and they were keeping him longer for observation. She assured me the test had gone without incident, but due to the medication he received for sedation, as it wore off throughout the evening, he could have uncontrolled body movements or seem drunk. Some effects were mild, and others were more pronounced; they would transfer Matthew back to his room soon. She assured me there was no reason for concern, and left.

The neurology tech had barely gone, when the team tapped on the door and wheeled Matthew in. He lay nearly still on the gurney, except for his head. He wobbled and shook his head oddly as if trying to shake an unpleasant thought. I cast the techs a questioning glance. It was the sedation medication wearing off, they told me.

The tech's description of his possible symptoms was an understatement. As he continued to wake up, he began flopping his body wildly from side to side, wailing, and flinging his arms. If left in his hospital bed, he could easily tangle himself in the tubing and wires connected to him or rip out his IV. I had no option but to settle into the teal vinyl recliner and do my best to handle him and keep him safe. Mom stood gaping, wanting to help but unsure what to do. It was late afternoon, and she needed to leave for home but hated to leave me alone, especially with Matthew in this state. I assured her I would be fine. I wasn't alone, I told her. There was an entire staff of nurses there to help me.

The cheeseburger sent by food service lay untouched under

the green plastic dome on the tray. She noticed that I hadn't eaten all day, and offered to take over so I could eat. I nuked it and took a bite, watching Mom struggle with Matthew. She did her best, but he was no longer a tiny baby and was quite unmanageable for her. The bite of a cheeseburger lay in a pasty wad in my mouth, and this thought dropped in my head with a dull thud: "Matthew is too much for her. She can no longer help me with him." The sinking reality dawned that I was truly on this daunting journey alone. Mark could help some, but worked nights and was simply unavailable for that reason. I had cared for the boys mostly alone and was exhausted at levels I'd never known. I swallowed hard, choking down both the gummy wad of cheeseburger and this heavily sinking reality. Seizures, new medications, and neurology clinic appointments were the stunning new reality. Seizures added another heavy layer to the weight I was already carrying. Matthew's needs were more intense than I first imagined. It all descended in a moment, like a crushing weight. There was nothing to do except push aside the chewy cheeseburger and take Matthew from my mother. This was primarily my road to walk. I had no choice but to push everything else aside, step up, and carry the load laid upon me. There was no cavalry galloping to my rescue. This was my life.

Within a week, we were home again but in an entirely different situation. Matthew would be on seizure medication for the foreseeable future, possibly for the rest of his life. He could have long periods of no seizures, but as he hit growth spurts or was ill, the seizures would most likely return. Seizures were now a part of our reality.

After Matthew's first onslaught of seizures and initial workup, we began regular trips to the neurology clinic, a protocol of seizure medications, and periodic EEGs. The basic EEG involved a day of home prep that required depriving Matthew of sleep for twelve hours before the scheduled test. The goal was for Matthew to have a seizure while asleep and hooked up to the machine so that the techs could document and pinpoint that seizure activity. Matthew's sleep deprivation required mine as well, as I had to ensure he did not fall asleep until the proper time.

The goal was to keep Matthew awake until the EEG techs had him prepped and ready to begin testing. In the testing room, a tech produced a bundle of EEG probes that she planned to glue to his head. Since Matthew was in perpetual motion, unless sound asleep, I was expected to hold him down while the techs glued the wires to his head. The tech produced a jar of pungent-smelling adhesive and explained the process to me. Through our previous barrage of tests and procedures, I'd come to know that if Matthew could hear my voice or see my face, he was usually calm in these intense medical situations. If I simply sang the songs he loved, he would often remain relatively calm, and quiet. So, as usual, I laid myself over him to hold him down, and softly sang of heaven and Jesus' love. The techs worked quickly and skillfully, pasting the probes to Matthew's head, and urged me to keep singing—saying "…it's different when you sing." They finished the bundle of wires with a gauze-wrap turban. I carefully repositioned him, allowing the bundle of wires to hang unobstructed, snuggled next to him on the hospital bed, and continued to softly sing his favorite songs. He often drifted off to sleep, and the techs recorded what data they received. When the techs decided they had gathered sufficient data, we roused Matthew. I laid over him again, singing of heaven and Jesus' love. The techs applied the solvent that released the probes. We packed Matthew up, got him home, fed him, and down for a much-needed nap. Most often, the data they gathered was minuscule; he never had "the big one" they were seeking while he was attached to the machine.

His seizures were often well-controlled for long periods, but disruptions like illness or teething usually threw him off-course. During those times, it was not uncommon for us to call an ambulance as his seizures would not stop, or he began to turn blue.

One rainy spring evening, Matthew's seizures escalated once again, and we called 911. I stood in the driveway watching the EMTs load Matthew into the ambulance. As the red and blue lights flickered and reflected on the wet pavement, this thought dropped into my mind: "My faith in God is my only safety net from a free fall into an abyss of despair. Jesus and this life of faith are all I have." Yet, I was finding in increasingly raw and real ways when Jesus was all I had, He was all I needed.

I knew the road ahead was a steep, uphill trek, more so than I anticipated. I considered myself a strong Christian, yet before Matthew's struggles, my faith remained untested. Now, a true crisis had arisen. Every day, it forced my faith into action. However, it seemed God needed even more from me if I intended to survive this arduous journey. The faith fortress I built in the barren place would become increasingly crucial. Even though faith, trust, and prayer were becoming my closest friends, more would be required. I desired strength and depth, but it became increasingly apparent that the route included even more difficulty. I shuddered at the thought, but the ambulance in my driveway was His confirmation.

At this point, I was confronted with a few options. I could choose to sink beneath the weight of this burden, resulting in self-pity and despair, becoming ineffective as a wife and mother. On the other hand, I could choose to arise and build, in God's strength. Standing fast upon that foundation of truth, I could continue working to build that impenetrable faith fortress. Weariness and desperation were all I had, yet He offered me more of Himself if I would press on.

Jesus offered strong, authentic faith through life-giving dependence upon Him. Matthew and Luke needed a strong, godly mother caring for them, raising them with compassion and skill. Choosing more of Him was my only viable option, so I dug deeper in an all-out pursuit of the strength He offered. Scripture became my lifeline and my prayer life was transformed into a soul-sustaining connection to my divine power source. The Holy Spirit became my tutor, Scripture became my textbook, obscurity became my schoolroom, and heartache became my schoolmaster. Through the practice of spiritual disciplines, I continued to cultivate the skills of a faith warrior. He began to teach me to defend the fortress of my mind by wielding the sword of His Word with power and waging war in prayer. This became my way of life.

The image of a flourishing tree in an unforgiving landscape has always intrigued me, and though the tree mentioned in the passage in Jeremiah 17 is planted near a stream, it still intrigued me. Since I lived in a barren place, I was challenged and encouraged to be more like that tree. Its secret, of course, was its water source. Because the tree took advantage of the readily accessible water supply, it was well-nourished and fruitful, even in drought. It remained unmoved and unaltered whether circumstances proved pleasant or painful. I longed to be like that fruitful tree.

Never before had I experienced such deep disappointment, confusion, and soul pain. Never before had I so needed to be the strongest and most courageous version of myself. Yet where could I find the healing comfort of His massive arms to steady me? How could I rise in strength and courage while in such pain? I turned to the only source of true strength and comfort I'd found. I dug deeper still into the Scriptures.

As I stayed in Scripture, I realized that stronger faith grows like a stronger muscle. However, the exercise required for building faith is simply this: acting upon the truth available in His Word, the Bible. It means acting upon what we read and understand, through faith, with little other confirmation than our trust in the One Who has spoken. We step forward in faith, based on our firm confidence in God's character. His character undergirds His trustworthiness. I often found He desired that I move forward in faith despite a sense of His closeness. Rushing winds, goosebumps, or the mysterious appearance of birds were not prerequisites for my obedience. He had already spoken in Scripture, and in faith, I must follow.

Following in faith like this felt akin to stepping onto a single steel cable stretched across a vast canyon, guided only by His unseen hand. Trust in His character was my only safety net. In those scenarios, the only way I found to survive the trek across those proverbial canyons was by locking eyes with my Savior and never looking away. Step by step, I'd walk forward into the swirling mist, guided by His Hand and sometimes only His Voice. Sometimes He went silent and simply illuminated the next step. Even so, as He revealed the next step, that was evidence of His presence. Along the way, I found that my trust in Him grew stronger with each trip across those mist-enshrouded canyons. It was as if with each act of faith, with each step into the mist, following His voice and taking His unseen hand, I laid another layer of steel cable to my faith bridge. I could take that faith bridge with me to the next canyon crossing. With each canyon crossing, my faith muscle grew and my trust in Jesus grew, not because circumstances were turning out well, but because I knew He was in control and His way was best, although it made no sense now. He would work all things out for our good and His ultimate glory, in His time. Yet at the time, I lived much of my life suspended at dizzying heights over these mist-enshrouded canyons, following His voice, reaching into the mist for His Hand, and watching for illumination of the next step.

Matthew's needs continued to be intense; his care was hands-on and exhausting. He took his first steps at two years old, yet was also busy and active. He also demonstrated no safety awareness and was often in danger of falling as he learned to climb (and did so with amazing speed). He also tended to mouth his hands, put things in his mouth, and engage in self-stimulating behaviors, accompanying special needs. He often flapped his hands and arms and incessantly kicked his legs. His First Steps therapists taught me helpful techniques to avoid those self-stimming behaviors. They also taught me how to calm him with massive rice and bean bags my mother made for us, and by using manual deep pressure. If I missed the early signals of an oncoming bout of overstimulation, it wasn't uncommon for me to spend nearly an hour unwinding him through weighted blankets, bean bags, and manual deep pressure.

Our mornings were filled with back-to-back therapists, periodic clinic or doctor visits, and the day-to-day activities accompanying life with two active toddlers. Like other moms of toddlers, doctor visits were frequent as both boys suffered from the usual upper respiratory maladies and ear infections. We were scheduled for tonsil and adenoid removal as soon as they were old enough. Luke's tonsils touched one another in the back of his throat when he wasn't sick, but nearly closed off his airway when he was. As a result, Luke also suffered from sleep apnea, which required my constant vigilance. Matthew's ear infections were frequent and intense. With several ear infections, he was inconsolable until his ear drum burst, releasing both the pressure and mustard-colored goop. The boys had their tonsil, adenoid, and ear tube surgeries when they were two years old. My heaviest concern leaned toward Matthew's recovery. However, it was Luke's recovery that went awry and landed him in the hospital. He refused to take pain medicine and then refused to drink or eat due to the pain. He quickly became dehydrated and the pain worsened. It seemed odd that he needed me since my attention was primarily on Matthew. Mark stepped in to stay with Matthew while Luke and I spent most of the night at our local urgent care. Luke was hospitalized and spent the following day in the hospital getting his pain and fluid intake under control. Once we were over that hurdle, Luke was quickly back on track. Ironically, Matthew skated through his recovery with ease.

Like all mothers of toddlers, my days began early and ran well into the nights. Sleep was a commodity; the workload was heavy and constant. Mark and I often passed briefly in the kitchen each morning as I was prepping for our first therapist and he was returning from work. I was glad to have the company of Matthew's therapists and my "pastor friends" on the radio. My Jesus was my ever-present Help in surgeries, illness, and the mundane, for He was equally Lord of it all. In the midst of this, my prayers began to shift.

Gone were the days of lobby attempts toward God. Though I kept praying for Matthew's healing, whether He healed Matthew or not was His business. My trust and commitment to Him did not depend on whether circumstances improved. If He never changed my circumstances, I would still follow. I found out daily, in intensely raw ways, that He was trustworthy. Even though I didn't understand or like what He was doing, I found I could rest in Him. His Word informed my trust with countless examples of saints who lived lives marked by painful and confusing circumstances, yet persevered in faith. Like many of them, I was doing everything I knew to do, yet daunting circumstances remained. However, God's plan was not immediate deliverance but crushing, strengthening, and rebuilding. This process repeated itself, not to leave me crushed and bleeding, but to remake me into a masterpiece that can only be formed through such trials.

FOOD FOR THOUGHT:

1. Has God ever dropped a massive weight upon you? What was your response? How did Scripture give you strength and perspective?

2. How would you describe your prayers lately? Have your prayers changed in recent days? How?

CHAPTER 4

CRYING OUT; RISING UP

"Trust in him at all times, O people; pour out your hearts before him; God is a refuge for us."

Psalm 62:8, ESV

"If your law had not been my delight, I would have perished in my affliction. I will never forget your precepts, for by them you have given me life."

Psalm 119:92-93, ESV

It has been said that hard times create strong men and strong women. My life increasingly resembled hard times–hard times that were not going to end any time soon; hard times that were likely to increase in difficulty as the boys got older and Matthew's needs continued.

Though I had already become much stronger in my ability to trust God, to persevere in faith and gain strength from His Word, I needed more. I needed to go deeper with God. I needed to not play around in the shallows. I needed the deep dive. My life circumstances required it if I planned to survive this journey with my faith intact. I needed all of Him that He was willing to give me.

I continued to absorb the psalms and pour out my raw, unfiltered emotions like the psalmists. As I did so, I noticed a pattern present in many psalms. After pouring out his grievances to God, the writer would settle into a quiet stillness, sometimes marked by the Hebrew word, "Selah." Then, the writer would remind himself of God's character, how He came through in the past, and His promise to never abandon us in our difficulties. As the psalmist continued reciting these truths to himself, a song would arise from his soul—praise, peace, and worship, despite terrible circumstances. Like me, the psalmists faced unending hardships, with no hope of relief or support on the horizon. I identified and took up that pattern as my prayer and heart cry. My prayers shifted from asking for an easier, happier life to requests for strength to persevere, wisdom to understand, and peace despite the storms. I continuously asked for Matthew's healing and perseverance in faith, but my happiness, joy, and peace no longer depended upon a change in circumstances.

As I camped in the Psalms, I noticed how prayer and worship are inextricably intertwined. Echoing the psalmists, I recognized that my initial outpouring of raw emotion would ultimately lead me to a profound reminder of His unchanging love, kindness, and unwavering faithfulness. The more truth I mined from Scripture, the more evidence I gathered to support the many ways I found Him faithful and kind in the daily grind. As I reminded myself of these truths that re-stabilized my faltering soul, a hymn of praise would simply arise from my soul like many psalmists. As often as I engaged in this practice, whether through the tattered scrap of a quiet time I could grab, over a sink of dirty dishes, or while feeding or calming Matthew, He was there to calm and quiet my frenzied soul.

I sunk my roots deep into Scripture and found a stunning scenario in Exodus 34. Moses is up on Mount Sinai with God. He asks to see God's glory and God agrees to reveal Himself, but only His back, as it would be too much for Moses to see His entire being. God covers Moses in the cleft of the rock and passes by, proclaiming His name and nature. After that encounter, Moses was different. His face glowed, and some said his hair was likely snow white. Following that experience, Moses took up the practice of meeting with God in a tent outside the camp each day. Astoundingly, the Cloud that dwelt over the Tabernacle would move to that tent where Moses was; God and Moses talked together in that tent as Friend with a friend. That was the kind of relationship I needed with God if I wanted not just to survive but thrive under challenging circumstances. I suffered no delusions that I shared equal status with Moses, but I certainly needed Him in the deepest way possible, just like Moses did. I had to create my own tent of meeting and see if God would meet me there in a deeper way—with even more of Himself. Although no shekinah glory filled my dining room, God did meet me there. His Word became my ongoing delight, as I feasted and drank deeply of His living water. I began to know the breathless wonder of dwelling with Almighty God. There was a deep, quiet peace residing within me that calmed and stabilized me. An abiding intimacy between us became as natural and vital as breathing. Like Joshua, I too, found it unthinkable to leave that tent of meeting, made holy by His presence.

I've always loved hymns; their depth challenges and moves me. When the boys were babies, I decided to sing hymns for them as their lullabies as an additional way to pour truth into them from infancy. Because of the sleep disturbances that often accompany special needs, it was most often Matthew I was desperately trying to get to sleep. Matthew's sleep disturbances persisted and necessitated my hands-on attention whenever he was awake for several days. Day after day, and night after night, I would sing hymns, as much for my benefit as his. As I sang, I sunk my roots deep into the truth in the hymn lyrics and applied the truth to our situation. My prayers melded with the hymns I sang, becoming my ongoing heart's cry.

As I sang: *"Day by day and with each passing moment, strength I find to meet my trials here . . ."* I lifted the stresses of that day to my gracious Father—the trials of Matthew's ongoing needs and pressing on through exhaustion day after day.

As I sang: *"Trusting in my Father's wise bestowment, I've no cause for worry or for fear. He whose heart is kind beyond all measure gives unto each day what He deems best."* I leaned hard into His sovereignty and lovingkindness. Though my heart was continually breaking for Matthew, his struggles with eating, sleeping, and special needs, I pressed my weary soul into Jesus. Though I didn't understand His ways, I knew He was infinitely good. He had a purpose in this season of pain, and He was working out His plan even as I rocked in my rocking chair with Matthew on my lap. As I sang, I pressed my cheek against Matthew's head, fingering his wispy brown hair. Whether he slumped against me in sleep or not, I sang on:

"Help me then in every tribulation, so to trust your promises, O Lord. That I lose not faith's sweet consolation offered me within your holy word. Help me, Lord, when toil and trouble meeting, e'er to take as from a father's hand, one by one, the days and moments fleeting, till I reach the promised land."

How often I wept and worshiped in the darkness while rocking Matthew on my lap. I knew that God promised to show up when we praise Him. I needed His presence, so I sang softly in the darkness, trusting Him to hear my prayer. I lifted the lyrics as a prayer or battle song and found Him ever-attentive to my voice, and sweetly present as I sang on in the night.

I lifted the lyrics as my prayer and heart's cry. I asked Him for strength to go on, to keep trusting Him despite my soul pain. I asked Him for wisdom to understand and for His help in staying on the pathway of truth and not slipping away into despair.

One early morning, I sneaked to the dining room to meet with God over strong coffee and my open Bible, continuing my trek through Philippians 4. Its admonitions to rejoice in the Lord, live free of anxiety, and walk in the peace that passes understanding frustrated me. I stood there in my floral PJs, steaming mug of coffee in hand, as I read and re-read the passage. As I read, I breathed this question into the dimly lit dining room as a frustrated prayer: *"How, how do I live above the anxiety? How do I rejoice in God and live a life marked by peace that surpasses understanding?"* I sat down to reread the passage, and a light of understanding dawned. In a moment, I connected the dots that linked the peace surpassing understanding with the content with which I chose to fill my mind, what I dwelt upon truly shaped my thought patterns. The route to that surpassing peace was as simple as altering the content I allowed into my mind. It was doable, and the victory I sought seemed finally within reach. I began a more intensive push to memorize Scripture, internalize it, and fill my mind with truth rather than unhelpful noise.

Shortly after I made that simple, yet stunning discovery, God showed me another great truth. It made an enormous impact and flung open the door to real spiritual victory. I refer to it as finding "ground zero" in the Christian battle because it was as if I unearthed an elusive, carefully guarded secret to true spiritual victory.

The "ground zero" secret that I discovered is this:

True spiritual growth and victory were possible to the extent to which I proactively engaged in the ongoing practice of renewing my mind with the truth of Scripture.

Since Scripture is God-breathed, ingesting it infuses everyday Christian people with God-breathed words of truth. These living words infused me with God's power, the power to think differently, the power to make different choices, and finally experience true victory. In this power, I could fight and win the battles I fought daily against fear, discouragement, and despair. I could be a strong and courageous truth warrior as I cared for my boys with humbleness and grace. As a result of that revelation, I began an even more intensive push toward renewing my mind. It was as simple as filling my mind with Scripture and allowing it to perform its transformative work in me. I also used the truth of the Bible to directly isolate, target, and combat the specific lies I'd come to believe, specifically lies about my worth in God's eyes. I began to memorize Scriptures that directly countered those lies with the truth. I often heard myself repeating those lies, like a video loop on repeat. I could stop the video, neutralize the lie with memorized Scripture, and redirect my mind to the truth. I found that more truth ingested equals more inner peace and more victory. On the flip side, less Scripture ingested equaled less inner peace and less victory. It was simple, but not easy. I knew I was in a war, yet I had always fought defense. Now I could fight offensively and finally win. This stunningly simple discovery made me realize that becoming an armed and dangerous swordswoman of truth was entirely possible. Spiritual strength, stability, and victory were well within my grasp if I fought lies with the truth of Scripture. The task before me was becoming a valiant swordswoman of truth, fighting for my survival, as well as my boys', despite the formidable circumstances in which we lived. I would love to say I strode forward in victory each day, but that would be a lie. Whenever I practiced the truths that I was unearthing, victory and joy were present. Whenever I neglected those truths, I quickly slumped into despair and defeat.

From time to time, Matthew's neurologist ordered an EEG, and on other occasions, they upped the ante and ordered a telemetry EEG (this type of EEG creates a video for a more accurate assessment of brain function). Once again, they were trying to pinpoint the point of origin for the seizure activity in Matthew's brain. The day-long prep preceding each telemetry EEG was the same as for the basic ones, except I had to pack and plan for us both to stay in the hospital for up to three days. The procedure was the same: the same smelly adhesive, the same expectation that I hold him down and sing songs of Jesus and heaven, as the same techs pasted the bundle of wires to his head and wrapped his head in a turban. However, with a telemetry EEG, I always had to keep Matthew in full view of the video cameras. The techs also provided me with a hand-held buzzer so I could document what I recognized as seizure activity on my end. The nurses provided Matthew with an appropriate kid-sized wheelchair to provide him with a different and more secure position other than rolling or flopping about on the hospital bed. I worked hard to keep him entertained and in full view of the camera. I sang for him and tried to read him stories. Nurses brought us toys and put movies on for us, but he showed no interest. Ultimately, I continued to sing for him, praying as I sang. Within a day or so, the techs decided they would not get the data they sought, so they forwarded their recommendations to the neurologist, suggesting we suspend the testing.

Matthew's therapy continued through First Steps. We did our best to follow the therapists' suggestions, as we were eager to do anything to foster Matthew's progress. One of his therapists suggested placing a full-length mirror lengthwise, just above baseboard height, to encourage Matthew to interact with himself in the mirror. We did so, yet Matthew's response was minuscule. They also suggested a makeshift ball pit in our finished basement for deep pressure and other benefits. An inflatable kiddie pool and plastic balls sufficed, and Luke and Matthew enjoyed it. Therapists also advocated for us to receive adaptive equipment, including large therapy balls, a platform swing, weighted blankets, and a special feeding chair that helped keep Matthew firmly supported for eating.

First Steps therapists also recommended hippotherapy for Matthew. During our weekly treks to hippotherapy, Luke and I watched Matthew tottering atop the massive horse, secured in a special seat. The therapist brought a CD of children's songs that Luke dubbed the "horsey songs." As the therapist led Matthew around the arena atop a horse, Luke climbed on the straw bales in the barn or played with the barn cats. He and I often strolled around petting other horses or walking the field roads around the stable. Luke loved the "horsey songs" so much that he begged me to buy a CD, and I was glad to oblige. Playing that CD of "horsey songs" became a regular addition to most days from that point forward. We often played the "horsey songs" during other therapy sessions, as we tried our best to find something that would pique Matthew's interest and prompt speech or interaction. Luke enjoyed the visits from therapists, who kindly involved him as much as possible to help Matthew.

Despite the skill and coaxing of our various First Steps therapists, Matthew remained nonverbal. He also continued to engage in many sensory-seeking and stimming behaviors. Matthew continued his hand-flapping and spinning, mouthing his hands and random objects. I had to remain vigilant to keep small objects inaccessible to keep him from choking. Often, when I tried to pick him up or carry him, he arched his back and flung his arms and body weight backward, making transporting him nearly impossible. Other times, he nestled against me nicely as I carried him. Therapists taught me skills and methods for meeting his sensory-seeking behaviors and heading off episodes of overstimulation. Sometimes I could head off an impending round of overstimulation; other times I did not. In those latter cases, I did my best to implement those skills to alleviate his behaviors and provide him relief.

On our final day of hippotherapy, my parents came for dinner. They planned to arrive shortly after we were scheduled to return from hippotherapy. I planned a simple menu and although the timing would be tight, I would be fine. Luke and I walked around the field roads and stables, petting the other horses and waiting for Matthew to be done. Despite my warnings to avoid the piles of horse poo, Luke stepped directly into one, covering his shoes in foul-smelling goop. I sat him on a stump, and took off his shoe, wiping it in the grass as best as possible. I put his shoe back on; as a farmgirl, it wasn't my first encounter with animal poo, so I decided to drive home with the windows down and clean him up once we were home. Matthew's therapist brought him to me, and we loaded up for a fragrant ride home.

One of my church friends called as we pulled out of the stable drive and onto the gravel road. She wondered how my day was going and asked about the boys. I told her I was headed home from hippotherapy, about Luke's "poo shoe" and my parents arriving for dinner within ninety minutes. She offered to help me. I was floored. She said she would meet me at our house and help me. When I pulled in the drive, she pulled in behind me. I gingerly lifted Luke out of the van, set him in the grass, and flipped his shoe off. He hobbled into the house with one shoe on while giggling with my friend. I hauled in Matthew and worked out a plan of attack. My friend brought Luke's shoe into the house, carrying it by the strings and wrinkling her nose at the smell.

"I'll tackle this," she offered. She began wiping his shoe with bleach wipes and disappeared into the bathroom, Luke following with keen interest. Luke and my friend were working away on the poo shoe, so I sat Matthew in his feeding chair for a snack while I started picking up the house and getting supper. I checked on my friend. She had scrubbed the horse poo from Luke's shoe and was cleaning my bathroom. She smiled at me in the bathroom mirror as I tried to protest. "It's something I can do to help you," she said as she wiped down the counter, tossing the bleach wipe into the trash. She hugged me, grabbed her purse and keys, and waved as she walked down the driveway. I returned to Matthew in the kitchen and finished his snack as I browned hamburger and started water for pasta. I was humbled and grateful for her kind-hearted selfless service. Her hands-on help allowed me enough time and space to catch my breath, fix a quick meal, and be ready when my parents pulled in.

Matthew aged out of the First Steps program when the boys turned three and transitioned to half-day preschool. The First Steps therapists submitted their reports and the teachers from Matthew's preschool scheduled an in-home visit. The morning of the visit, the troupe of teachers filed into our living room, seating themselves in a circle around the room. Matthew toddled curiously about from person to person, sometimes plopping into a lap and then getting up again until he settled with me. The teachers were kind and seemed undaunted by Matthew and his needs. We talked about the various therapies and services he'd received through First Steps, and would receive in his classroom. We received his start date and everything was a go. His building was less than a mile from our house, so I drove him rather than having him ride the bus. Luke also started preschool at a local church. Matthew would attend four days per week for half days, and Luke would attend three days per week for half days. That meant for three days each week I had three hours of freedom. Matthew's school was released before Luke's, so I would drive to Matthew's school to pick him up and then drive to Luke's school to retrieve him. Matthew and I often walked the hallways together as we waited for Luke, as he was always on the move and it was easier to allow him to walk than to try to handle him in a crowded lobby.

Matthew continued having feeding issues and needed textures he could easily handle, so I prepared his snack for school each day and either sent it in his backpack or drove it up to the building before his snack time. Cornmeal mush was a texture and taste he loved, so I made it often for his snack. I liberally laced it with butter and brown sugar to give Matthew extra calories. Luke referred to it as "Matthew's yellow cereal" and the name stuck. Luke liked it as well and often requested it. I made it often for the boys to share.

Luke began making friends, learning, and thriving at his preschool. Each Thanksgiving, the preschool had its version of a Thanksgiving feast. I was asked to bake cornbread mini-muffins and pumpkin mini-muffins for their feast and cookies for the reception following the Christmas program; Luke and his two friends made an adorable trio of Wise Men for the pageant.

As Christmas rolled around, Luke and I baked massive amounts of cookies to make generous trays for teachers, Matthew's therapists, neighbors, and friends. He often stood on a chair at my side, helping me stir and mix ingredients, and was always up for a taste test. We opted for a table-top Christmas tree to accommodate Matthew's inquisitive hands. He could see the lights and sparkles, but couldn't reach them, so it was a good option for the time being.

When the boys turned five, I determined I should try my best to have a proper birthday party. Luke could invite his preschool and church friends; he'd been asked to several of his peers' parties, and it seemed I should allow him the same pleasure. He wanted an "army men" theme so I planned "army man" themed games for an outdoor party in our backyard. I sent the invitations in his school backpack and handed them out at church. I made chocolate cupcakes, crushed cookies to resemble dirt, and topped each cupcake with an army guy. The weather was sunny and perfect, until forty minutes before the party. One of our fast-moving midwestern fronts brought a bone-chilling wind and pouring rain. We moved the party indoors and skipped the games as parents and children crammed into our living and dining rooms. I showed the kids the ball pit in our finished basement—the one we used for Matthew's therapy, and they were thrilled. I was gratified that I had tried; Luke was thrilled he'd had a real party. Matthew seemed glad when the commotion was over.

Luke often accompanied me to ladies' Bible study at our church during his non-preschool days. I took advantage of the childcare, and I was thrilled to have the opportunity to re-engage. As I interacted with the other ladies, I found my faith walk was different than theirs—not better or worse, just different. I wondered if it reflected the intensity level at which I lived and how His Word was my lifeline to Him and the Holy Spirit's power. I sought out opportunities to serve and was soon baking coffee cakes and cinnamon rolls for refreshments and filled in as table leader whenever our regular leader was gone. I felt my heavy load lifting and repositioning just enough to think again of those dreams of writing, speaking, singing, and teaching. At His request, I'd released them into His care years ago, and there they remained. He would return them if He wanted me to have them back now. I didn't want to push or grasp for them, I had to patiently wait for His time and way. In a quiet corner of my mind, the farm girl in her orange sundress nodded in agreement.

We continued to attend church as a family, doing our best to maintain as much normalcy as possible. Though each church outing was an exhausting, emotional ordeal for me, we needed to make the effort to attend for all our sakes. While at the church service, I spent much of my time settling Matthew and giving him snacks and meds. The time I spent in worship service was limited, but like an exhausted deer, I stopped momentarily to drink deeply from the refreshing stream of worship songs and truth. Church allowed me to interact with others, and sit momentarily without the boys clamoring for my attention. I drank deeply from the refreshing strength-infusing practice of corporate worship. The worship songs and hymns we sang in corporate worship mingled with those I sang at home during the week, and rose from my battle-weary soul as my ongoing prayer and heart cry. When we could attend our small group, I drank deeply of the friendship and fellowship. It was the highlight of my week.

On one occasion, a group of moms from our church community group organized a playdate at an indoor play area at a local shopping center. The boys and I were invited, and though I knew it would be daunting given Matthew's needs, I packed up the boys, and we went. Luke and his friends climbed and played on the oversized fruit in the play area. Matthew was fascinated by the oversized fruit and wanted to explore it. Given his cognitive deficits, he needed my constant assistance and was unable to play appropriately with the other children. His presence and disabilities began to make both him and me a spectacle and annoyance to the other children. Luke was enjoying himself, and it was good for him to play with his peers. I continued to struggle to keep

Matthew entertained and out of the way. The other moms sat at a distance chatting and watching their kids play. As the playdate wound down, the kids gathered around tables in the play area sipping juice boxes and munching fish crackers. I handled Matthew's snack a safe distance away from the others. As I loaded up the boys and drove home, I remember thinking how that playdate encapsulated the path I walked with the boys. I tried to do what was best for Luke and Matthew, but their different needs kept me forever in an awkward stretch. Matthew's needs necessitated my hands-on presence, while Luke needed me in different ways. That stretch also pulled me away from the social contact with other moms I desperately needed. The loneliness accompanying me to the playdate came home like an unwelcome guest. It stood ready to remind me that *it* was my only friend and would always be that way. The fact that Jesus was my powerful, tender and ever-present companion kept me on solid footing.

With the boys near the end of preschool, I began peering ahead toward their diverging paths as we hurtled toward kindergarten. Matthew's school life would be non-academic. If we stayed in our current district, Luke could likely attend a building different from Matthew, and both would be bussed some distance from our house. There were also no guarantees that Luke would not land in in a notoriously bad building within our district. Moving to another district was the only way to ensure Luke's best outcome.

Mark and I began the difficult conversations, weighed the various issues carefully, and decided to leap. Early in 2006, we started the arduous process of getting our house ready to sell. Mark began painting during the evenings while I got the boys to bed. While the boys were in preschool, I spent my precious free hours cleaning out closets, hauling junk to the Goodwill, and deep cleaning. We put the house on the market in March of that year. Like homeowners with less challenging circumstances, the house had to be kept show-ready. Our stress load became nearly unbearable with two preschoolers, Matthew's special needs, and Mark's night schedule.

I knew we were making the right decision to move, but our many challenges loomed large. I prayed as I worked: I prayed for God to bring the right buyer to us, the right home in the right location, the right floor plan that would be safe for Matthew, and to place Luke in a neighborhood school with peers. I prayed through each intricacy and laid it all before God. Despite my prayerfulness, the tension within our home was thick and heavy.

Because of Matthew's special needs, leaving the house for an afternoon was a major undertaking. To eat, he needed to be in his adaptive feeding chair. His incessant hand-flapping, spinning, and mouthing his hands and random objects made us a spectacle in public. In spaces with fluorescent lighting, his sensitive ears picked up the constant buzzing. As a result, he often yelled, hit himself in the head, or flopped his body side-to-side. Bystanders gaped or eyed us with quiet pity. Luke was a handful in his own right. He was a typical rambunctious and delightfully playful boy. I opted instead for parks in pleasant weather, drives in the countryside, or an impromptu visit to Mark's parents.

I continued to pray as I kept our house show-ready. The tension was unrelenting. I knew if I could simply get alone with God and talk it all out with Him, I would get clarity and peace. There was no time, except after Mark left for work and the boys were asleep, so I asked Him to help the boys sleep so we could talk. The boys went to bed, and Mark left for work. I got ready for bed and settled in for a long conversation with my Jesus. If it took all night to pray it through, I was prepared for that. I had gone many nights with little sleep and knew how to make coffee, so I started the in-depth conversation with Him I'd needed to have for months—if not years.

I sat on the bed as we talked through all the stress surrounding our move, as I'd been praying for months. I lay on the bed and bawled as I poured out my heartache and disappointment over Matthew's ongoing needs. I ranted into the bathroom mirror over the mounting tension between Mark and me surrounding our move. I sat on the bathroom floor whispering to the Ancient of Days of unhealed wounds festering within me—leaving no stone unturned. There was nothing unsaid between us; there was an openness, a deep communion. Although He gave no answers, there was a quietness about me. I had said it all; He had listened. My heart's cries had been heard within the portals of heaven. It seemed as though I'd opened a holy door that few had opened and crossed into a space few had gone. I hesitated to go to bed lest that door click shut somewhere at night and never reopen. I knew that notion was foolishness; I had just found the pathway to that holy door through prayer. I could walk the same path again at any time. I sat on the bathroom floor for a long time, basking in His presence until He urged me to bed. I slipped beneath the covers, still talking to Him as I drifted off to sleep.

Despite the difficult circumstances, we got an offer on our house and prepared for house-hunting. Due to Matthew's needs, only certain floor plans were viable options for us. We needed no open stairs or balconies, so split entries were off the table. We were looking for a raised ranch with a fenced backyard. We also needed a property in a neighborhood and away from busy streets. We must ensure Matthew's safety if he bolted away from me.

For some of our house-hunting excursions, our friend Teresa watched the boys. Other times, church friends were happy to watch Luke, but we had to bring Matthew along. When Matthew was with us, Mark and the realtor would look at the house first and give their assessment. If the house was a viable option, he would stay with Matthew in the van as the realtor walked me through. After several fruitless excursions, we found one house that would work. It was a raised ranch with no open stairs or balconies. It was in a family-friendly neighborhood with a yard and even a small garden spot. The clencher for me was a clump of yellow and purple crocuses in the flower bed at the base of the porch railing heralding the beginning of spring.

We made an offer and waited. Later that evening, we saw Teresa at church and realized the house we'd just toured, on which we'd made an offer, was two doors away from hers. We had no idea, but our Lord did. He knew what we needed, and where we needed to be. Mark and our realtor exchanged calls and texts throughout the evening. Before the weekend was over, our offer was accepted. We prepared to move. Mark handled the inspections necessary for selling our house, and we are ready to close on our new home.

Matthew became increasingly agitated and curious as I packed and the stacks of boxes mounted. He knew something major was happening, but couldn't ask the obvious questions tumbling over one another in his mind. On moving day, we had a three-hour window to make the transfer while the boys were in preschool. My parents planned to help us; Dad brought his truck and a flatbed trailer.

It was the boys' final day of preschool. Matthew's school was having a water day, so I packed his trunks, towel, and extra clothes, thankful that he would be tired when I picked him up. I took Luke to his school and rushed home to meet the movers. My parents were waiting in our driveway. We immediately got to work, loading the trucks and making a speedy transfer. Once at our new house, I laid out lunch for Mark, and my parents and I raced, first to Matthew's school and then to Luke's, bringing them both to the new house. When I got Matthew inside, he ran up and down the hall and in and out of all the rooms, wide-eyed; full of questions he could not ask. Mark and Dad got to work installing baby gates at the head of the basement stairs and over the doorway to Matthew's room. Mom helped me start laundry and unpack the kitchen before they left for home. I followed our same evening and bedtime routine and Matthew seemed to understand that this was our new home. His family was with him in this new place, and all was well. He relaxed and even slept in his new bedroom without difficulty.

Our massive endeavor was complete, and we were in a new place, both literally and figuratively. The boys would start kindergarten in June in our new school district as summer school began. Luke was both nervous and excited. I was concerned for Matthew's well-being in a new school district with new teachers and paras. I sat with the boys on the front steps waiting for the school bus with a sick knot in my stomach. The yellow school bus barreled around the corner and within moments, both boys were aboard. My life was in a different place once again. I sat on the front steps for a long time as tears streamed and soaked into my shirt. The sick knot in my gut settled in for an extended stay. I had already planned a school trip when Matthew's class ate lunch to ensure their adaptive chairs would serve his needs. In the cafeteria, I found Luke in line with his class and noticed blood stringing down the front of his shirt. He saw me, and thrust forward his open palm; a bloody tooth lay in his hand. He proudly displayed his toothless grin. As his class moved on, he cast me a wistful glance, squinted tears away, and was gone. In my preoccupation over Matthew's first day of kindergarten, it was also Luke's. He missed me; he needed me. On his first day of kindergarten, he'd lost his first tooth. I squinted away my tears, as pangs of guilt and sadness jabbed my heart. I checked again on Matthew and went home to a strangely quiet house.

The transition to our new house was done. I had heard in programs on my Christian radio station that major life transitions like a move could prompt a reset within the family. In these resets, the family would reassess and re-evaluate their situation. Family members often developed a newfound appreciation for each other as they saw one another in a different light and bonded together to make a fresh start in their new location. I was hopeful our transition would prompt such a reset for my family—a reset that would lift the heavy load I carried, alleviate my isolation, or shorten my stay in the barren place somehow. However, Mark returned to work within days, and I continued caring for the boys as before. All that changed was our address. It was the same old routine in a different location. Yet my Jesus was with me still, and the same life-giving truth poured into a different kitchen through the Bible teaching on the same kitchen radio.

It quickly became obvious that my sojourn in the barren place would not be short-lived. It would be my dwelling place indefinitely. There would be no family reset; there would be no reprieve. There would be no new-found appreciation for my endless work or stress. There would be no lifting of the heavy load I carried, no steps to alleviate my isolation or shorten my stay in the barren place. I would have to settle in for the long haul.

The loneliness and isolation that had become my constant companions at our old address, accompanied me to our new address and moved in for an extended stay. I spent my days in our new house as I had in our former home. The boys' care occupied my days, and often my nights. As before, I went for weeks barely speaking to another adult besides Mark.

As before, it was my job to continue building that proverbial stronghold in my Midian-like surroundings—the one I'd been building since the boys were babies. The truths I learned and re-learned were the building materials and the fortress itself. Jesus was my divine Companion as I continued to build. He was my divine Guide, Foreman, Architect, and Friend. He would continue to protect and provide for the boys and me in this faith fortress in the barren place. As before, He would continue to infuse me with His power, strength, and wisdom as I cared for Matthew and raised Luke.

We began exploring our new neighborhood during our first summer in our new house. The park near our home, the playground, the bike trail, and the creek offered opportunities for outings, and we took as many trips as we could manage with Matthew's needs. My dad gifted the boys with a green and yellow John Deere wagon. I loaded Matthew in the wagon and Luke rode his bike as we explored our new park. Sometimes Matthew sat nicely in the wagon enjoying the ride. Other times he quickly became agitated by the movement, bucking and flailing about in the wagon or trying to stand up or climb out. Sometimes he simply wanted to get out of the wagon and walk as I held his hand. Other times he was triggered by the movement and often became unmanageable. In such cases, we had to cut our outings short and head back home.

We knew Matthew loved playing in the water, and our yard also offered that opportunity. Even though water-play was an exhausting, two-person job, Matthew's joy made it worthwhile. He couldn't play as typical children would; he giggled and squealed, kicked at the sprinkler, and tried to sit on it or carry it around!

Attending church as a family continued to be an exhausting and stress-filled ordeal. Even so, it remained the highlight of the week for me. I spent much time settling Matthew in the nursery, but I had a little company and conversation. When I could attend worship, I drank deeply from the refreshing stream of corporate worship, lifting the songs as both declarations and battle cries.

During the dog days of summer, the boys and I were simply at home together. Matthew developed a means of securing my undivided attention by a practice I can only describe as "climbing me." He would grab, pull at me, and try to climb up me like I was a tree. His goal was to either get me to pick him up or sit on the floor so he could plop into my lap. One hot summer afternoon, I was in the kitchen washing dishes, listening to another Chuck Swindoll sermon on Christian radio. Matthew was hanging out with me in the kitchen and began his attention-getting practice of climbing on me. As I washed the dishes and listened, Matthew's clamoring won out, and I sat on the kitchen floor, leaning back against the dishwasher. Matthew gleefully plopped into my lap, and I snuggled him there as I listened to Dr. Swindoll's sermon. To my surprise, it was the same sermon series I had listened to when the boys were babies—the one that had been so impactful. Dr. Swindoll spoke again of Joseph enslaved in Egypt, Ruth gleaning in grainfields, and Moses in Midian. As I nestled Matthew on my lap and listened, I watched the play of light and shadow against the kitchen wall as tree branches outside waved in the hot wind. God confirmed the realities settling upon me since our move as I listened. The barren place was my home now and would be for the foreseeable future. As I sat there with Matthew wriggling in my lap, the tears began to spill down my cheeks—tears for Matthew's struggles and needs, and my loneliness and sadness. This barren place was my Midian: Matthew's needs, Luke growing up, this endless, exhausting work in this forgotten pocket of the world. However, even as I sat on the kitchen floor, in another droning afternoon in the barren place, my Jesus assured me that just as He had not forgotten Moses in Midian, neither had He forgotten the boys nor me. A sweet, sad, resting peace flooded me as I sat there. This was His special place for me now, just as it had been all along. I could rest in the mundane dullness, for He was in that too. I found that I could rest in that truth and trust Him to make this dullness beautiful through His presence.

FOOD FOR THOUGHT:

1. Have you ever had a no-holds-barred conversation with God as I describe above? How was it helpful? How did it feel?

2. Does God have you in a barren place right now? Why do you think He's placed you there? What is He saying to you about this season?

CHAPTER 5

MY ROCK OF REFUGE IN THRASHING WATERS

"The eternal God is your dwelling place, and underneath are the everlasting arms."

Deuteronomy 33:27a, ESV

"Save me, O God! For the waters have come up to my neck. I sink in deep mire, where there is no foothold; I have come into deep waters and the flood sweeps over me."

Psalm 69:1-2, ESV

Summer waned, and the boys were slated to begin full-day kindergarten in the fall in the new school district. I received the parent emails and mailers regarding Back-to-School night with all the dates and times listed. I knew I would have to bite the bullet and take the boys, but I also wanted to avoid the crowds if possible for my sake and Matthew's. I chose a time as early in the evening as possible, got everyone ready, and drove them to the school. I needed to meet both teachers, so we met Luke's teacher first. She was a veteran teacher, exactly the sort of teacher he needed; one unruffled by his typical kindergarten boy behavior, yet also gently uncompromising in expectations for classroom behavior. He toured the classroom, found his cubby and name card at a table, and snapped a photo with his teacher. Then, we were off to Matthew's classroom. His teacher was unavailable, and the classroom was locked and dark. However, I had met his teacher during summer school, so I was comfortable with things going as well as they could. As we snaked through the hallways and into the congested parking lot, the building began bustling with parents and excited children. I loaded the boys in their car seats and quickly exited, glad to check that massive endeavor off my to-do list.

Because of Matthew's special needs, he and Luke were placed in a building outside our neighborhood that could more adequately handle Matthew's needs. Both he and Luke would be bussed to that building across town. It wasn't a perfect arrangement, but it worked for now. The first day of the new school year rolled around and Luke was nervous and excited. The night before, we picked out Luke's clothes and shoes and laid them out. He wondered where he'd eat lunch and where he'd go to the bathroom. I reminded him of the bathroom in his classroom and the lunchroom we'd walked by. He helped me pack his Spiderman lunchbox, set it in the fridge, and laid out his backpack. We followed our evening routine. As usual, I hustled Matthew through the bath and let Luke play in the tub with extra bubbles, animals, and army men. I toweled Matthew off, diapered him, and dressed him in fresh pajamas hoping he'd sleep, yet knowing there were no guarantees he would.

I continued the evening routine by reading library books, a Bible story, working on a memory verse, praying, and singing a hymn or two. Thankfully, Matthew drifted off to sleep, and Luke did as well. I slipped away into the quiet kitchen to finish the dishes with a mixture of emotions swirling in my head. I was stunned that my baby boys were truly starting kindergarten. I was happy for Luke; it was his natural next step. I was sobered and nervous for Matthew and full of unanswered questions that required a 'wait and see' approach. There was nothing to do but send him to school and see what happened. I re-checked the bus schedule and gamed out my morning plan, gauging how long it took to feed Matthew, give his meds, and dress him in school clothes. I checked and rechecked both lunchboxes and decided to call it a night. I lay in bed staring into the darkness, praying over my boys and this monumental step we were all taking. This was a massive step into their next phase as elementary school children, and for me as a mother to elementary school boys. I was releasing both of my precious boys into the care of others. I was confident Luke would do well and was in good hands. I was less sure about Matthew. I again laid my concerns before God's throne and drifted off to sleep.

I woke before my alarm the next morning and slipped out to the kitchen to make coffee and start my morning. I checked and rechecked the bus schedule to ensure my well-timed game plan was on track as I finished laying out Matthew's clothes, shoes, and backpack. I knew Luke would be up, dressed, and full of nervous excitement as soon as he heard me in the kitchen, so I worked as quickly and quietly as possible in my morning routine. True to form, as soon as I clunked a skillet too loudly, Luke appeared in the kitchen doorway. Our first day of school routine had begun. I got Luke his breakfast, keeping an eye on the clock for when I planned to wake Matthew to start his school day prep. I made him a bowl of maple and brown sugar oatmeal that he loved, laid out his meds, and went to get him up. Luke dressed and worked through the routine we discussed as I began feeding a very sleepy Matthew his breakfast and giving his meds.

I finished feeding Matthew, cleaned him up, and dressed him for school. I packed the boys' backpacks and rechecked the time and bus schedule as we waited for the bus. I walked them outside as we waited on the driveway for the bus. Luke played in the driveway while I sat with Matthew on my lap and waited for the bus with heaviness in my gut. The yellow-orange school bus turned into our street, stopped at our driveway, and the boys were aboard. I smiled and waved nervously to the bus driver as he closed the door. I stood watching and waving as the bus disappeared over the hill, tears stinging my eyes. I sat on the steps for a few minutes letting the reality sink into me. There was nothing left to do but go inside, start cleaning up the breakfast dishes, and move along with my day. I got a cup of coffee and sat in my strangely quiet house. It was my first cup of coffee in a silent house since June when the boys started summer school. I drank in the quietness and the coffee with an odd, unsettled feeling. I longed to relax into this new-found quietness, but didn't dare allow myself that luxury—I didn't trust that it was truly mine or that it would last. I was also concerned for Matthew. However, the moment was mine for now, so I thanked God for it, drank my coffee, and read my Bible in peace for the first time since I could remember.

I moved through my day in quiet, yet nervous anticipation. I kept myself busy with housework, laundry, and cooking and al-lowed myself the luxury of a solo trip to the grocery store. I made a nice lunch for Mark and me and got him off to work forty minutes before the boys' bus time. I cracked the front door as I worked to finish the lunch dishes, clean up the kitchen, and prepare an after-school snack for the boys as I watched for the yellow-orange bus to round the corner. Right on schedule, the bus pulled into our street, stopped at our driveway, and opened the door. Luke bounded down the steps, up the driveway, and into the house. A para helped Matthew out of his seat, handing me his backpack as he nearly fell down the bus stairs. As I carried him up the drive, stairs, and into the house, I could smell his wet diaper.

I immediately changed him; it was clear by the diaper's weight that he had not been changed all day. I counted the diapers I'd sent in his backpack that morning; they were exactly as I had put them. I called Matthew's teacher and left a message. I got the boys snacks and drinks and moved into our new after-school routine. Luke was content to watch Animal Planet while I fed Matthew his snack. After his snack, Matthew followed me around as I worked or hung out in the kitchen as I fixed supper. Day One of the boys' elementary school years was in the books; everyone survived. We moved smoothly through our evening routine and both boys fell asleep quickly after an exhausting first day of school. As I finished washing the dinner dishes, cleaning up, and packing lunches, I thought of Matthew sitting all day in his soggy diaper. I decided to add a Sharpie mark to his diaper in an inconspicuous spot in the morning when I dressed him. If he came home in the same diaper again, I was prepared to do more than leave a message on his teacher's voicemail. I quickly wrote a note about his unchanged diaper in Matthew's take-home folder and stuck it in his backpack.

The following morning, I added a Sharpie dot to his diaper near the bottom, diapered, and dressed him for school. Once again, he came home in the same diaper. I called the teacher again, and called the principal, leaving a message on his voicemail. I determined that if it happened again, I would call the principal and go there myself to see what was happening in Matthew's classroom. On the morning of Day Three, I wrote "Change My Diaper" in large letters with my Sharpie on the back of Matthew's diaper as I dressed him for school. The more I thought about him sitting all day in an unchanged diaper, the more upset I became. By mid-morning, I could no longer stand it and went for an unannounced visit to Matthew's classroom. I checked in with the secretary, who buzzed the classroom to let the teacher know I was on my way down. When I entered the classroom, a para was changing his diaper. Matthew seemed pleased to see me at school and came to me for hugs and kisses. The para had read my message on Matthew's diaper and nervously laughed as we briefly conversed. I strongly suspected that had I not made the unannounced visit to the classroom, Matthew would've continued to come home unchanged until I spoke face-to-face with the principal. However, my visit to the school ended the situation, and I was grateful, although I continued to be uneasy about his placement. I kept my eyes and ears open for issues. I was determined to befriend the paras in Matthew's classroom, volunteer, and be a frequent visitor to ensure he was not neglected.

With the boys in full-day kindergarten, I finally had a chance to catch my breath, read my Bible, and clean my house. I joined a ladies' Bible study at church and began volunteering in the boys' classrooms. Mark woke up mid-morning, so he and I had unhindered time together that we hadn't had since the boys were born. I often made us a nice lunch to share before he went to work. I could pack his lunch and see him off before the boys came home. I began to work out a more organized house-cleaning routine and relax into the role that I loved as a stay-at-home mom.

For Matthew, the school year was liberally peppered with upper respiratory illnesses that gave us frequent flier status in the doctor's office and the ENT clinic at our children's hospital. Matthew received the diagnosis of Eustachian tube dysfunction from his ENT doctor. The diagnosis helped explain his ongoing ear issues and required that he always have functional ear tubes. Sometimes I knew when the old tubes fell out, and other times I wouldn't know until he developed an ear infection. If Matthew had an ear infection when his ear tubes were functional, they could be managed with antibiotic ear drops and over-the-counter pain reliever. When his tubes were not functional, he was inconsolable until his ear drum finally burst, releasing both the ear pressure and yellow goop. Each nasty ear infection sent us back to the ENT clinic where we restarted the loop of a new set of tubes and another trip through same-day surgery.

About halfway through the boys' kindergarten year, Mark asked what I planned to do now that the boys were in school. I mentioned how grateful I was for the reprieve and how I enjoyed being able to attend ladies' Bible study. I could just clean, cook, and be home, which was all I wanted. Besides, Matthew's care continued unabated and Luke was certainly all-boy and a handful in his own right. I didn't pick up on his hint.

The boys' birthday arrived in late October, complete with Luke's favorite meal, homemade chicken and noodles, homemade rolls, and chocolate cupcakes, which he liberally decorated with candy corn and candy pumpkins. My parents came for a birthday visit, and that made the day extra special for Luke. Luke always blew out the candles for him and Matthew and opened his gifts and Matthew's.

Following the boys' birthday, the holidays swept in like a whirlwind. Since I had more freedom than I'd had in years, I took advantage of it and baked enormous amounts of cookies and candies for Luke's teacher, Matthew's teacher, each of the classroom paras, and Matthew's therapists. We put up the Christmas tree in our finished basement so Luke could enjoy the tree without Matthew knocking it over. I decorated the archways with evergreen garland and red bows and carefully looped and secured any trailing ends safely out of Matthew's reach. As always, our holidays were different due to Matthew's needs, but we did our best to make the holiday as normal as possible for Luke while appropriate and special for Matthew. We hosted Mark's family for Christmas dinner, so the workload was enormous, but I was used to a heavy workload. Baking, cooking, and hosting lay directly in my wheelhouse, and provided a positive outlet for me, despite the work.

Matthew was always active and mobile, which was both a bane and a blessing. I was glad he was active and mobile, however, his lack of safety awareness continued unabated. As always, without my constant vigilance, he was often in peril within moments, requiring that I remain within arm's length of him at all times. He was a fast climber, often quickly in danger from climbing on tabletops, dining room chairs, or the back of the sofa. He frequently crammed something into his mouth, and the possibility of choking was imminent.

As he got taller, he could reach the stovetop or kitchen knives. Restricting Matthew's access to the kitchen became a matter of urgency. It quickly became apparent that we needed to install full-length, windowed doors blocking off any kitchen access for him. Matthew could be in the kitchen with me but had to be in his wheelchair to avoid catastrophe. Though he was small for his age, he was all arms and legs at times. Amazingly, he could nearly clear the kitchen countertop with a few arm-swipes if within reach. Unknowingly, he often sent drinking glasses splintering across the kitchen floor or flipped mail or open cookbooks onto the floor. He was often in danger of flinging hot casserole onto himself or the floor—or both. We found a contractor and installed the full-length doors as quickly as possible.

Matthew and I often hung out in the kitchen together; he was in his wheelchair, and I was prepping meals or cleaning up. However, when I wasn't working in the kitchen, he and I were confined to the house's living room. He spent his time "stimming." When "stimming," he was constantly spinning to the left while extending and retracting his hand in a figure-eight pattern while making a swooshing noise—it was his "default setting." However, he would often stop spinning to watch the hummingbirds at the feeder in the flower bed outside our tall windows. The male hummingbirds often flew directly up to the glass, challenging their reflection in the window. He would often back up to me, and plop into my lap to watch them. Matthew and I often got mesmerizing close-ups of the tiny, shimmering creatures' eyes, tongues, and beaks just a window-pane distance away.

With each cold season, Matthew got sick, as most kids do. Ear infections were a constant issue and ear tubes were replaced every other year. We were seen in various clinics at our local children's hospital on a routine basis, including neurology and ENT. When he got sick, his seizure threshold broke down and the seizure activity escalated. Often, I managed with a trip to our primary doctor, or the Diastat (sedative) that we always carried with us. However, it was not uncommon for Matthew and I to be in the hospital for several days, or even week-long stays. Mark would take time off work whenever possible, get Luke to school, and maintain as much normalcy as possible. As always, our church family rushed in with a steady stream of casseroles to keep Mark and Luke fed while Matthew and I were away. Church family came to the hospital to keep me company, bring me coffee and chocolate, listen, and simply be present in my pain.

Frankly, our daily life ran at ridiculously high levels of exhaustion and stress that often left me tightly wound and high-strung. I did my best to handle the intense stress, but honestly, my exhaustion and loneliness usually led me to discouragement and despair. I often felt I was hanging on by a thread, and my heart cries continued to echo the same rawness of the psalms.

Life in the barren place had become a much longer ordeal than I first imagined. It was filled with daily drudgery, loneliness, and struggle that no one witnessed but Jesus. Though I despised being a complainer, I also knew that a complaining spirit grows naturally in our hearts, as brambles grow in untended soil. When the boys were babies, I'd learned that cultivating gratefulness is key to combating a complaining, bitter spirit. Despite the harsh climate of the barren place, I did my best in His strength to cultivate a grateful heart. However, looking around at my circumstances, I found ample reason for discouragement and complaining. Still, as often as I followed the template marked out in many psalms, I found great cause for gratefulness.

This truth hit home late one night as Matthew's sleep disturbances kept him overstimulated and wakeful. Since I had to be near him if he was awake, I lay beside him on his bed, desperately wishing he'd fall asleep, and growing increasingly grumpy. Then I heard the Holy Spirit's nudging whisper, "…He inhabits the praises of His people." I certainly needed Him, and if praising Him was a route to His presence, my task was obvious. There in the darkness, I began to pray. Frankly, in my weariness, I had to ask God to show me reasons for gratefulness. Matthew lay beside me incessantly rolling side to side, kicking my legs, so I began to thank God that both Matthew and I had legs—his were functional, and so were mine. It seemed stupid, but He prompted me to continue. I thanked God for basics like the bed where Matthew and I lay, the house where we lived, the kindness of church friends, food, clothes, and the like. Within moments of pushing forward through what seemed like a ridiculous exercise, a dam began breaking in my spirit, and I began to sing softly. I sang, *"Jesus, name above all names…*

Emanuel, God is with us..." I certainly needed God with me that night, so by faith, I kept singing, lifting the lyrics as a prayer as I sang. My heart rose in worship. Gratefulness spilled over along with my streaming tears, as I worshiped alone in the darkness.

Soon, I noticed Matthew's body was calming, so I sang on, listening for the deep, rhythmic breathing of sleep. Finally, it happened; he was asleep, yet how I wanted to stay there in that sacred space. I had just demonstrated to myself that He truly does inhabit the praises of His people, so I knew the route to that sacred space and could return there again through thanksgiving. I gingerly slipped out into my bed, but a powerful truth firmly landed that night. His presence is always with us but is accessed more deeply through thanksgiving. I also learned that pushing forward in thanksgiving, even though it seems ridiculous, truly leads to His deeper presence. Thanksgiving was the pathway to peace, as I'd discovered when the boys were babies. This pathway, which had become well-worn earlier, was still the right path. The old truths were still the right ones.

The new year rolled in, the boys returned to school, and I was grateful after the holiday break. Life returned to its pre-holiday cadence. Once the boys were on the bus, I spent my mornings tip-toeing around so I didn't wake Mark. I learned how to do exercise videos on mute, and perfectly timed the laundry to beat the buzzer on the dryer. I often prepared a nice meal for us to share for lunch. During one of those lunches, Mark asked me once again what I planned to do now that the boys were in school. Ire rose within me. "He's not going there again, is he?" I mused. He was.

The conversation that followed was ugly, and a turning point in our marriage. He stated his long-term plan that I would return to the workplace once the boys were in school. I stated my long-held desire to be a stay-at-home mother. It seemed the only fitting place for me given Matthew's needs. The realities of Mark's work schedule meant I handled those tasks mostly single-handedly.

I pointed out the issues of childcare for two children and the added complications of Matthew's special needs. I pointed out how I had been out of the workplace for seven years and the many ways in which the workplace had changed in that timeframe. I would be thrown into an environment where I was expected to know and understand computer-based tasks outside my skill set—the learning curve would be too steep, and I couldn't even operate at an industry baseline.

Those concerns were seemingly brushed aside. I was expected to find a job that would accommodate child care for the boys and bring in whatever money I could to help meet our mounting financial needs. When school started again in the fall, I was expected to find a job.

My stomach clenched into a fist. The hurt and anger simmering within me over the years rose to a rolling boil. It seemed my endless work in caregiving for Matthew, and raising Luke had been dismissed as unimportant because it did not bring financial dividends. No matter his intentions, the message that landed with me was that my worth and value to Mark were based upon my earning power, which was meager at best. It landed firmly and stuck to my soul like Velcro. The more I tried to pull it loose, the more firmly it clung to me. I was crushed.

My mind raced in anger and confusion. My untended soul wound festered, seeping its poison into our already-strained marriage. My anger gave the evil one all the foothold he needed to stoke the smoldering coals of hurt and anger into a raging blaze of resentment. Mark's concern for our finances was valid. He was the sole breadwinner for our family and our medical bills were astronomical and ongoing with no end in sight.

I hunkered down in prayer. I prayed for some way to respectfully honor his request and still remain afloat physically, emotionally, and spiritually. My Jesus had carried me through many sudden twists in our road, I was sure He would make a way for me here as well. I was praying for a miraculous intervention and for Mark to change his mind. However, once again, His way was not circumventing the impending difficulty, but providing me the strength, grace, and courage to walk directly into the difficulty in His strength.

On the last day of summer school, Matthew's class enjoyed a water play day. Matthew's teacher marveled at how he loved the water. I agreed and mentioned how he did remarkably well with a floatie in the pool. She suggested we meet at her subdivision's pool and spray park so Matthew and Luke could enjoy the water and have an outing. I agreed and we made our plans. Matthew squealed with delight, running up and down, pausing to hold his hands directly in the highest pressure point of the spray. His teacher and I supported him as he played in the pool. Luke played in the pool with her children. As we dried off and sat in the lounge chairs, she mentioned a job opening in her classroom for a paraprofessional. It was full-time, but could be part-time after the first semester. I agreed to look into it. I would have the same hours as the boys. I knew how to care for children with special needs, as I cared for Matthew. It was worth a try.

I dragged my resume out of mothballs, updated it, and filled out the online application. I was immediately hired. I was alternately stunned, terrified, and sick to my stomach. I was sure this endeavor would not go well. The first day of school arrived and I was unceremoniously thrust into Matthew's classroom, and the care of other special needs students. I was well-versed in the hands-on care of special needs children and quickly became attached to the children. I also had the benefit of co-workers. For the first time since the boys were born, I had fellow adults in my daily world. I was amazed at how I'd missed adult interaction and loved the camaraderie. My coworkers were amazed by the homemade treats I brought to school and my resilience. It wasn't uncommon for one of them to look me in the eye and ask if I was okay. There were some benefits, but the exhaustion was unreal.

In the special needs classroom in the school environment, I was able to see how Matthew's needs compared with his peers those of his peers in the self-contained classroom. District officials and I restarted the conversations about a transfer to a special needs school. I was open to the possibility, yet wanted to make the best decision for Matthew without being cornered or coerced. The special education department assured me they would do their best to serve his needs, so Matthew remained in our local school district in a self-contained classroom for the time being. I was in his classroom daily and could keep a watchful eye on the situation. I was Matthew's only advocate and desired to make the best decision possible as I was his only voice. My hands-on role within the school district positioned me more effectively as his advocate, and this became another one of my roles as his mother.

With me back in the workplace, several things changed at home. The intensity level of my circumstances was immediately ratcheted up several levels. Running on empty had become my way of life since the boys were born. Now I ran on caffeine, adrenaline, and fumes during the day and soldiered through the exhaustion and massive workload in the evenings. Soldiering through while running on fumes became my way of life. I took the boys to work with me, cared for other special needs kids during the workday, and took the boys home with me after work. The situation worked from a scheduling standpoint. However, it simply extended my exhausting and high-stress circumstances into the workplace and removed any vestige of a reprieve. Matthew's sleep disruptions did not magically end with me working. Some nights he remained wakeful despite my best efforts at a bedtime routine and calming deep pressure. Those nights when he "pulled an all-nighter" simply meant he and I both went to school exhausted. He could nap as needed; I could not.

I was struggling, but still on solid footing. I was firmly tethered to The Rock of Ages, yet mercilessly thrashed by the waves in that sea of difficulty, wildly grasping for the solid ground I knew would stabilize me. I was clinging to Jesus for my very survival. I was working hard to employ those skills and disciplines I had learned when the boys were babies. I was struggling to stay afloat in this increasingly churning sea of exhaustion and difficult circumstances. My deep soul-wound continued to fester, devolving into smoldering anger. I was shocked, stunned, and angry that this difficulty was seemingly forced upon me with what felt like a lack of regard for my well-being. This smoldering anger seeped poisonous contempt into our marriage, marring what little time we spent together.

Sometimes my exhausting and difficult circumstances converged with my festering soul-wound, sweeping me into a whirlpool that threatened to suck me under. The loneliness and heartache I'd known all along were often my only companions. The evil one lurked like a vulture, awaiting my demise by exhaustion and discouragement. However, it remained imperative that I not succumb to the demise he awaited. I needed to continue building a strong and sheltering faith in this barren place, not only for myself but for my boys. I must defy what was quickly becoming a death-like place by continuing to marinate my soul in Scripture and drinking deeply of His life-giving stream. I knew what I must do to stay afloat, and as I stabilized my soul with Scripture, remarkably, I was able to do so. The waves, however, did not stop beating me, and I was often underwater, bobbing to the surface gasping for breath, and then tossed about in the waves again and again. However, I kept crying out to Jesus. He often plucked me out of the waves, it seemed, and set me on bedrock, restabilizing me. Other times, He set me in a protected cleft as the storm howled about me. However, He never left me. He showed me again and again that He was with me—He was doing something in me through this raging tempest.

During the school year, our evening activities were driven by Matthew's med schedule and need for routine. Like other parents, I also helped Luke learn his sight words, math facts, and spelling words. At bedtime, we often piled into Matthew's bed with our Bible storybook, memory verse cards, hymnal, and a stack of library books. I would read the Bible story, we'd work on memory verses, and sing a few hymns.

As I sang, ". . .*whatever my lot, Thou hast taught me to say, it is well, it is well with my soul,*". I reminded myself that "my lot" for this night was caring for my boys alone after a full day of school. My Jesus was teaching me every day to look to Him in trusting obedience through this heavy workload and sing out in full-throated praise despite my overwhelming circumstances. *"It is well, it is well with my soul."* If I truly believed He is always working out His perfect will, I must believe it now, and sing on through the darkness and pain.

Matthew often drifted off to sleep before we ended our hymns. Luke and I would read library books in his bed until he fell asleep. Once the boys were asleep, I began washing dishes, doing laundry, cleaning bathrooms, and making lunches for the next day. In my exhaustion, I forced myself to complete the next step of each task, and then the other.

One evening, I was making a PB&J for Luke's lunch as I listened to a sermon on my kitchen radio. I forced myself through each step of the process, as I often did. I held the jar of peanut butter in one hand and the knife in the other as I prepared to spread more peanut butter on the bread. I couldn't think what to do next. My pastor-friend on the radio sounded far away. I felt myself slipping, fading—my hand plunked into the peanut butter bread on the counter, the goopy knife bounced onto the floor, and the jar of peanut butter spun wildly across the counter. Had I nearly passed out and collapsed from exhaustion? It startled me, but similar episodes began happening again and again with increased regularity.

At the end of the first semester, I met with the school principal, requesting part-time employment. He had already been approached by another para in a nearby classroom with the same request; we were able to work out a job-share arrangement that temporarily solved both of our problems. I worked three full days per week, and that allowed me to accommodate Mark's request that I contribute financially while maintaining a sane workload and stress level.

Matthew remained in our local school district, though his teacher and I continued our discussions regarding his placement at a more appropriate school. He was with a teacher and paras who did their best to care for him while openly admitting the current school setting could not accommodate his needs. We began preparations for Matthew's transfer to a special needs school, started the evaluations, and called the necessary IEP meetings to make that a reality. Mark and I toured the new school and met his teachers and paras. I met several of Matthew's classmates, and their needs compared with his. This was where he belonged. The paperwork was submitted in the spring, which began a long summer of waiting.

Matthew's transfer was completed just days before the new school year began. I was sad, yet relieved, as he was where he belonged. His needs were profound, but he was in capable hands.

Though I couldn't be with Matthew at his new school, Jesus prepared the way ahead of us. Matthew's para was a kind and capable Christian lady named Ms. Pamela. She was undaunted by his messy neediness and showed both skilled and tender compassion toward him. Ms. Pamela and Matthew became special friends at his new school. As she recognized a need within our family to care for him, she stepped in to help. She secured a wheelchair suitable for his needs, which doubled as an appropriate feeding chair. It also rolled nicely into the kitchen doorway so I could include him, talking to him as I worked. Ms. Pamela was also willing to watch Matthew so Mark and I could grab a rare date night. She was even willing to stay overnight to allow us an equally rare getaway and stepped in to provide respite for me.

As in their preschool days, I once again had two boys with very different needs in two different school districts. Because the boys were in different districts, Matthew's bus time crisscrossed with release times at my building. I made special arrangements for Matthew's bus to drop him off at my building, and he and I waited out the final moments of my work day getting loaded and waiting for Luke in the van. Within Matthew's first year at Maple Valley, it became increasingly clear that both Luke and I should change buildings within our same district. It would place Luke among neighborhood peers and would be a short walk from our house. Matthew's special needs placed us in our current building, and with him at a different school, there was no need to stay. Mark and I talked it through while the boys were in school; Mark deferred to me as I worked in the district and was close to the situation. I dreaded having the conversation with Luke, as he'd made friends within our building, but I knew it was better to make the change earlier rather than later in his elementary school years. I braved it and broke the news to Luke. Predictably, he wailed and begged me not to do it; but I explained it to him and listened to his concerns. I assured him that though it may be hard at first, he would be okay. I put in for a transfer for us both to the new building. The paperwork was submitted and Luke's transfer was complete. Luke would start summer school at our new building. I would start in the new building in the fall.

Life was changing rapidly, but we were each where we needed to be. Matthew was secure at his school. Luke was where he needed to be, and though my work situation was not optimal, I too, was where I must be. I still shouldered the massive weight of Matthew's care, raising Luke virtually alone, while working in a high-stress environment, but being part-time made it doable. Mark remained on the second shift, which allowed him to be home during the midday, but pulled him away during the evenings. Increasingly, we lived in two separate worlds. The boys and I carried on in our world of school and home life. Mark carried on in his world of work, with weekend and holiday interactions at home. I did my best to bridge the gap between the two worlds. However, it was becoming an ever-widening gap.

FOOD FOR THOUGHT:

1. When life circumstances are unrelenting and difficult, how is God giving you strength to stand fast? How is He comforting you? How is Scripture helping?

2. How do you handle change? What steadies you when life seems to be spinning out of control? What role do Scripture, worship, and prayer play in that process?

CHAPTER 6

PERSEVERING IN OBSCURITY

"And let us not grow weary in doing good, for in due season we will reap, if we do not give up."

Galatians 6:9 ESV

"Humble yourselves, therefore, under the mighty hand of God so that at the proper time he may exalt you, casting all your anxieties on him, because he cares for you."

1 Peter 5:6–7, ESV

"Do the next thing. I don't know any simpler formula for peace, for relief from the stress and anxiety than that very practical, very down-to-earth word of wisdom. Do the next thing. That has gotten me through more agonies than anything else I could recommend."

(Elliot, Elisabeth. *Suffering is Never for Nothing*. B&H Publishing Group, 2019.)

It was the last day of school at the building where Luke was in second grade and I worked as a paraprofessional. As usual, Matthew's bus driver dropped him off at my building, where I met them at the front door. As I walked Matthew across the parking lot to our van, he stiffened, teeth clenched, and dropped to the ground convulsing in a seizure. I waited until it passed, mentally noted the type and duration, and carried him to our van. I laid him on the floor of the van and waited for Luke. Matthew began seizing again. Luke emerged from the school, swinging his backpack, and basking in the glow of the last day of school. I said nothing to Luke about Matthew's seizures, loaded the boys, and maneuvered past the busyness of the car-rider line, creating a game plan in my mind. The first step was to get us all home as quickly as possible.

By the time we pulled in at home, Matthew was seizing again. I carried him into the house, called the neurologist's phone nurse, and left a message. I helped Luke with his afterschool snack and listened as he chattered about friends and last-day fun. As I listened, I kept a watchful eye on Matthew as I logged his seizure activity in the notebook on the kitchen table and waited for the neurology nurse to call back. Matthew's seizures continued.

Luke eyed Matthew, then me. He stood motionless, his hand deep in a box of cheese crackers. "Is Brother okay?" he asked.

"No Buddy, he's not," I said. "He's having lots of seizures."

"Will he go to the hospital again?" Luke asked. "Will Daddy stay with me again?"

"I'm sure Daddy will stay with you," I said. "I hope Brother doesn't have to go to the hospital again, but he's having a hard time." I repacked my hospital bag, logged more seizures, and texted Teresa two doors down. Within moments, she was tapping on the front door. Matthew lay on the couch, exhausted from seizing. I relayed the events of the past hour as we continued to map out a game plan if Matthew needed to go to the hospital. She offered to take Luke with her until Mark came home—the phone nurse from neurology called back. If Matthew had another seizure, she said to use Diastat and bring him to the emergency room. Before I was off the phone with her, he was seizing again. I told her I was using the Diastat and was bringing Matthew in.

"Is Brother gonna be okay?" Luke asked again, slipping on his camo crocs as he prepped to go with Teresa.

"I hope so, the doctors can usually help him," I said reassuringly. "Daddy will come get you when he comes home." I reminded Luke of Teresa's tropical fish aquarium and new puppies, hoping for a distraction. Teresa smiled reassuringly and the two of them started down the street chatting about the aquarium and puppies.

I texted Mark about the activities of the past hours and asked him to call me. I grabbed my purse, keys, and hospital bag, loaded Matthew into his car seat, and prepared for the trek to the emergency room. I dialed the emergency room and pulled out; thankfully a receptionist answered. Again, I explained the events of the past hour, relayed the recommendations from the neurology phone nurse, and that we were headed down upon her instructions. She agreed to be on the lookout for us. Mark called back; he assured me he would leave work and retrieve Luke from Teresa, and that he'd take care of Luke in my absence.

Because of the Diastat, Matthew was sleepy and dozed as I drove, parked, and lugged him up the hill toward the emergency room entrance. At the security podium, the guard took my ID and brought me a transport wagon as I waited for my adhesive ID sticker to print. I thankfully laid Matthew in the wagon and proceeded to the emergency room. I mentioned my phone call to the receptionist, and she escorted us to a side room. Matthew was waking up; the seizures started again. We were fast-tracked through the process and hospitalized once again. Matthew and I were settled into one of our regular rooms, and greeted by our usual nurses.

The neurologist ordered a stronger medication to stop his seizures, and the nurses started an IV. Matthew finally stopped seizing and was sound asleep. I gratefully settled into the pink vinyl recliner, waiting for whatever came next. I was growing increasingly familiar with being in the hospital with Matthew and was establishing a settling-in routine. The nurses brought bedding for me to convert the sofa into a bed, so I busied myself with that task. I called Mark with an update; he had already retrieved Luke from the neighbors. Thankfully, all was well on the home front.

I ordered a food service tray for myself for supper and looked forward to a quiet evening. As nurses came and went, they mentioned a coffee station in the elevator lobby down the hall. I wandered in that direction, finding an ample supply of both coffee and tea. My day was improving by the presence of simple joys like coffee, food, and the prospect of a quiet evening. I took my steaming coffee back to Matthew's room, and sank into the pink recliner, basking in the joy of a moment's rest, even if it was in Matthew's hospital room. The quiet evening materialized, even though it was coffee from the machine in the elevator lobby, and a hospital food service tray, I was grateful for it. Matthew was heavily sedated and simply slept.

The next day, the neurology team adjusted and re-adjusted his medications with limited success. Matthew was more wakeful as his sedation wore off. With his increased wakefulness, the seizures returned, although with less frequency. On the afternoon of the second day, two neurologists came to see us. The first examined Matthew and asked me questions as he always did, and the other stood quietly holding a stapled packet of papers. Then the first neurologist said they'd been studying Matthew's case, and were almost certain he met all the benchmarks for a diagnosis of a seizure disorder called Lennox-Gastaut. On cue, it seemed, the second neurologist handed me the stapled packet describing the condition. I carefully listened as they described the condition. There was no cure, but there were medications to mitigate symptoms. It was not a genetic syndrome, just a special type of seizure disorder. Matthew was already on the recommended medications; they would continue to manage and monitor symptoms. There was a strong possibility, they said, that Matthew's seizures could dissipate as he reached adolescence. There was also the possibility the seizures would become more frequent and intense, causing increased difficulty, and even death. They brushed that possibility aside, indicating they would monitor his seizure activity closely as he matured and hope for the best outcome. Within days, we were released with new dosages for the same medications, a diagnosis, and orders for another telemetry EEG. I was assured a scheduler from neurology would call me to set it all up.

In some ways, it was gratifying to have a diagnosis for one of Matthew's issues; in other ways, it felt like just another hospital stay. The diagnosis gave a name to one of his many issues; though it had a name, there was still no solution, no cure. Our life with Matthew continued to be a series of problems with few answers and limited solutions.

After resettling at home following Matthew's hospitalization, there was nothing left to do except get ready for summer school. His summer school ran half-day sessions throughout June. He attended a special needs school with a competent nurse on hand, and although the situation wasn't ideal, there was no reason not to send him on the bus to summer school. Matthew rode the bus with his special needs peers and sat directly behind the driver in his adaptive car seat.

Luke's summer often kicked off with a trip to church family camp. Church friends adopted him for Memorial Day weekend, as we were unable to attend given Matthew's needs. Luke loved church family camp, and our friends' kindness gave Luke an extended weekend of normalcy, the chance to make friends, and take the deep dive into nature that he craved. He often arrived home from family camp sun-tanned, exhausted, and famished, yet full of stories of good times at the lake.

After family camp, the remainder of Luke's summer was mostly spent with neighborhood friends. They rode bikes and played at the neighborhood park and pool. Since Luke always loved the outdoors, he was quite content to putter around the yard, park, and the nearby creek. He loved looking for squirmy creatures and enjoying the reactions they raised from the neighbor girls.

As the boys and I were home during the summer, Mark was more present for us all. Mark was able to watch Matthew long enough for me to spend a few moments tending my tiny garden and picking whatever crop was in season. One June morning I came in from the garden clutching double fistfuls of freshly picked green beans. Later that afternoon, those same beans plinked into the saucepan as I snapped them for supper. As I gazed up at my shadowy reflection in the kitchen window, I wondered what the farmgirl in her orange sundress would think or say if she knew the pathway her girlhood dreams had taken–the disappointment, sadness and heavy workload. As I finished snapping my beans, a tiny bean seed spurted out of a bean and onto my finger. I held it there, squeezing it gently. I watched as it began to crack beneath my gentle pressure– so like my girlhood dreams. I had released that girlhood dream into His care years ago, and if He was slowly crushing it, it was to transform it into deeper beauty and productivity, just like that seed. Just as the seed dies in order to produce its intended fruit, so the girlhood dream could endure His crushing if it meant the birth of something greater. The image lingered, surfaced and resurfaced as I went about my long summer days of caregiving.

Since Mark was home with us more, he was able to attend Luke's practices and games, but had to handle them alone as I was taking care of Matthew. He was able to help me with the heavy lifting involved in Matthew's care, like transferring him into his wheelchair, or helping me shower or bathe him. While he was available to help me with Matthew, the realities of Matthew's heavy, hands-on care were raw and ever-present for Mark, unlike during the school year.

I worked hard to take both boys to the pool whenever feasible. It gave Luke some normalcy and allowed Matthew the joy of being in the water. He would splash, play, and giggle heartily in a floaty and loved sprinklers and spray parks. Though it was an exhausting ordeal, Matthew's joy made it worthwhile. If Matthew was not in summer school, he and I would almost always be together at home. I did my best to break up the long, hot days with trips to the park. I would put Matthew in our John Deere wagon, and Luke would often ride his bike. Sometimes Matthew would sit calmly in the wagon, enjoying the movement. Other times he could not sit in the wagon and was increasingly agitated by the movement, arching his back and bucking wildly or rolling in the base of the wagon, flailing his arms and legs. Those instances cut our outings short.

As Matthew didn't know how to play with toys, he spent much of his time "stimming" as he followed either Luke or me around the house. Matthew loved music and my singing. He and I often hung out in his room while I played CDs of kids' worship songs or well-worn CDs of "the horsey songs." Our long summer afternoons were usually spent simply hanging out together, as it was next to impossible to accomplish most tasks unless Matthew was secured in his wheelchair.

The scheduler from neurology called to set up his telemetry EEG and everything was quickly arranged. As usual, Matthew and I would stay in the telemetry EEG unit at least overnight. They were waiting to catch "the big one" while he was hooked up to all the probes and in full view of the video monitors.

When Matthew was smaller, the task of keeping him relatively still was difficult, yet doable. However, as he got older and bigger and his behaviors increased, the task was still doable, but ridiculously difficult. As before, I tried my best to keep him on or near the hospital bed, in full view of the camera to eliminate more of these tests. When I wasn't feeding him in his feeding chair, both he and I were on the hospital bed together. Kind nurses offered toys and movies. Since Matthew didn't know how to play with toys, and showed no interest in movies, we were simply together on the bed. I prayed over him and sang the same hymns and children's songs I'd always sung for him. He "stimmed," dozed, or patiently sat in his wheelchair with the turban of EEG probes glued to his head. If I needed a bathroom break, I buzzed a nurse to sit with him. This pattern continued for two days.

One afternoon, I saw the EEG tech and a nurse talking quietly in the attached lab, and then the nurse came around beside the hospital bed to speak with me. She said the tech was not getting the data she needed. She also said they could see from the video footage that I was exhausting myself in Matthew's care while trying to keep him contained for testing purposes. She recommended ending the testing, sending us home, and would send that recommendation to the neurologist. I was relieved and gratified that someone saw how hard I worked caring for Matthew. Later that afternoon, as I signed the discharge paperwork, the nurse asked me if I had daily help at home for Matthew's care. I told her I did not, but assured her I did the best I could. "He's lucky to have a dedicated mom like you," she said, as we packed up to head home. It felt good to be seen and to hear her words of affirmation and encouragement. Caring for Matthew as I did was simply my way of life, and had been for years. Honestly, I never gave it a second thought.

As the summer droned on, I was often counting down the days to the beginning of school. Because Matthew's school was in a different district, his schedule usually offered me a few days reprieve. I could catch my breath, meet Luke's new teacher, settle him in his new classroom, and attend the staff meetings and convocation. I always looked forward to the few days' reprieve, yet hated returning to the classroom each year. I simply wanted to be home. I longed to breathe deeply, have a moment to think, sit and talk with my Jesus, and drink an entire cup of coffee.

"Do the next thing." It was a popular catchphrase in Christian circles at that time. I first heard it on a radio program entitled *Gateway to Joy*. I often listened to Elisabeth Elliot's radio program, as it was part of the daily programming on my Christian radio station. I often heard her say "Do the next thing," and wondered how it could help get me through my long days of caregiving, exhaustion, and isolation. I struggled to know what she meant, so I asked God to show me. Sometimes the "next thing" was washing a sink of dirty dishes. Sometimes it was making a casserole for supper or cleaning the bathroom. Other times, it meant I held Matthew in my lap as I sang to him songs of heaven and Jesus's love. I found it always involved praying.

That simple mindset of doing the "next thing" anchored me in the truth of 1 Peter 5:6-7. As I did the next task in humility and devotion to Him, I was humbling myself under God's mighty hand. If He chose to exalt me at all, that was His business. It was my job to serve Him in my kitchen and laundry room as I cared

for my boys with their very different needs. As I did so, I constantly prayed, and by doing so, I was continually casting my anxieties
upon Him. The communication lines between God and me were
always open and humming with conversation.

As I followed that simple instruction, I was learning to trust
Him on an altogether different plain. I had personal knowledge
and experience with the One Who was in charge. Because I knew
He had a plan and His plan was good, I could rest—I could be at
peace even though circumstances were heartbreaking. The path was
often confusing, convoluted, or just plain crazy, yet, I could rest
in my knowledge and experience of His heart, His ways, and His
undying Word.

As I went about my daily tasks, several words surfaced and
resurfaced in my mind. They bobbed about like beach balls that
refused to stay below the waterline though I pushed them under
again and again. They defined my days and often my nights. Those
words were perseverance, drudgery, and obscurity.

I found there is more to perseverance than simply gutting it
out for another week or month, and refusing to give up no matter
the difficulties. The deeper questions to me were *why* do we persevere, and *how* do we persevere? What deep truth do we learn as we
persevere?

I found I could persevere because my knowledge and experience with God affirmed that He is infinitely wise and powerful, and
more vast than any circumstance I faced. Though we are created in
His likeness, He is altogether different from us. His purposes and
methods are higher and more vast than ours and therefore, we will
not understand them, because He is not like us. However, I found
I could rest in His character as revealed in Scripture. My personal
knowledge and experience affirmed it as trustworthy. Therefore,

I found I could press on, because His Word informed me of His nature and His tender compassion. It also informed me of His vastness and transcendence. His Word spoke of a blessed hope, hope that is more than wishful thinking, more than a pathetic grasping for the sparkling vapor of "happily ever after"—it was a true and living hope made possible by our Savior's death and resurrection and sealed by His holy blood. His Word is true. Everything He promised, He will do. It will not make sense now; *He* will not make sense now because His ways are different, vast, and transcendent. Heaven is a real place, and real people go there. It is more spectacular and breathtakingly beautiful than our human words can describe. Because all of this is true, it gave me the strength to press on. I could see with eyes of faith what He promised in His Word, and knowing it was all true gave me the courage to carry on.

I also found I could persevere in adverse circumstances when I understood what was at stake should I give up. As I cared for my boys, it was incumbent upon me to stay strong in God's power because I stood in a strategic place in their lives. If I excelled, it could make all the difference for their care and well-being, but more importantly, it meant that my efforts spiritually had an eternal impact if I excelled at them in Jesus's name. The reverse was also true. If I shirked my duties, not only would my boys suffer neglect, but my lack of perseverance could have eternal consequences. So, I pushed forward despite my ongoing fatigue.

The other reason I pushed on through the exhaustion was because there was nothing else to do. There were needs to be met, and I was the only one to meet them. There was work to be done, and if I didn't do it, no one would. The boys' needs were ever-present, yet different. As their mother, it was my responsibility to meet them in His strength and wisdom.

People would often ask me, "How do you do it?" "I just do,"

was often my answer. Sometimes the answer is as simple as that. We do what we must to care for those around us. However, without the ongoing infusing power of the Holy Spirit working through me, I could never have carried on as I did. He gave me wisdom to see that my menial tasks had deep and enduring value as I did them in His name. As I cared for my two sons, I was serving Him in obedience and humility.

Without His infusing strength, I could have gutted it out for a season, and then collapsed in exhaustion and defeat. However, in His strength, I could do things I would not be able to do ordinarily. I was not superhuman, but I was infused with divine power and wisdom as I remained connected to Him. He was the source of my strength. In His strength, I could "scale a wall" as it says in Psalm 18. The walls I was scaling were not physical, but walls of discouragement and disappointment, coupled with Matthew's neediness, seizures, and the heavy demands of caregiving. Luke needed a mother to help him with his homework, take him to practices, and attend his ball games. He needed me to read him stories of magical places with talking animals, fair maidens, and brave boys who matured into noble knights. Mostly, he needed a kind and godly mother to read Bible stories each night, teach him to pray, and send him off to sleep upon the strains of a hymn. He needed those things whether I was exhausted or not, whether or not I was fighting hard against the clutches of despair. Even if I was overwhelmed or discouraged, he still needed those tender gifts a godly mother bestows. So, I prayed for strength to carry on another ten minutes and be fully present in those ten minutes for my son. In His strength, I sang the hymns, read the stories, and prayed the prayers. Often, I was rewarded with more of Him as He met me there in those tender moments. How often I lingered on Luke's bed long after he'd drifted to sleep on the wings of my prayers. The holy hush in the room was palpable—how could I walk away? I often remained as Luke's eyelids drooped and his breath came in soft, deep sighs, reading the psalms aloud to myself in the glow of light streaming from the hallway. The dishes could wait; this holy moment may never have come again.

Matthew also needed me; he was dependent upon me for his survival. If I didn't feed him, no one would. If I didn't give him his medication, no one would. If I didn't bathe him, dress him, and brush his teeth, no one would. He also needed a compassionate and strong mother who understood his various sounds and expressions and what they meant. He needed me to sing his favorite songs, to patiently settle him in his bed at night, or stay up with him if he couldn't sleep. He needed me to know why he couldn't sleep and to handle it if I could. He needed me to understand him and the words he could not say. He needed those things whether I was exhausted or not. He needed me to be patient and compassionate with his neediness even if I was overwhelmed, sad, or discouraged. He needed me to be a pillar of strength and stability that I could only be through God's strength. So, in His name, I asked for strength for another half hour to be Jesus for my son, understand what he needed, and fill that need in God's strength. So, in His strength, I sang the songs, provided calming deep pressure, gave him another drink, and lay beside him until he went to sleep. As with Luke, Jesus often met me there in the darkness. The same holy stillness often settled in Matthew's room as I lay listening for his deep rhythmic breathing. As I lay in the darkness, a prayer often rose—a heart cry of exhaustion and sadness coupled with a hymn of praise for His faithfulness on this hard road. God was with me this night, just like the others. He saw what I was doing when no one else saw, and He took note.

Obscurity was my homeland, especially in summer. Many

days I saw no other human besides the boys. I didn't talk to other adults for days on end. I went nowhere except to the mailbox. I carried on within my four walls, working in obscurity. No one else knew where I was or how I was doing. It often felt like no one cared. However, my Jesus knew and He cared. That knowledge and often kept me afloat in a sea of menial dullness, and never-ending work. No other human saw or knew what I did to care for my boys. As Matthew struggled through another feeding or I logged another seizure episode in the notebook on the kitchen table, no one saw the tears I wiped away on my faded tee shirt. No one saw or knew about the umpteenth mess I cleaned up. No one saw or knew how I was exhausted to the point of tears, and still had to keep going. However, my heavenly Father saw each act of selfless service. He knew.

As I worked, I pondered the lyrics to the hymns I sang over the boys each evening. *"He giveth more grace when the burden grows greater; He sendeth more strength when the labors increase. To added affliction He addeth more mercy; To multiplied trials, His multiplied peace . . ."* I was finding this true each day. In my multiplied trials, I drank deeply from the wellspring of His mercies, and received daily His manifold grace.

Menial work is humbling; it can crush us, or make us. There is something beautifully authentic about a person who isn't too self-important to scrub a bathroom floor or take out the trash. Menial work can separate the very fibers of our souls and show us what is there. If we allow Him to do His work in us, He uses seasons of menial work to purify us. As I submitted to my assigned place of caregiving and housework, I found a grounding peace and sweet communion with Him. He was at work in me. Where else but in obscurity could I learn to serve faithfully for an audience of One?

This point struck home one droning afternoon as I was prepping a meal for supper. Matthew sat in his wheelchair in the kitchen doorway, as usual. I half-listened to the sermon from one of my "pastor friends" on the kitchen radio as I prepped a casserole for supper. As I sauteed onions, stirred my pot of boiling pasta, and chatted to Matthew about what I was doing, my "pastor friend" talked about humbly serving an audience of One. Then I heard the pastor say, "God is equally present among the casseroles..." I eyed the greased casserole dish on my counter as I scraped the contents of my saucepan into the dish. Then the pastor said it again, "You may find yourself among the casseroles right now and wonder how God could be at work there." There I stood, dripping saucepan poised over the greased casserole dish, spatula in hand, had God just seen me here in this kitchen—among the casseroles? Had He just spoken tender encouragement to me through the pastor's words? Had He just filled my sagging sails with His breath? Had He just buoyed me on the updraft of confidence that His holy eye rested upon me? The pastor's words underscored this truth: He accepts our humble, obedient service as an offering whether it's on a foreign field or at home among the casseroles. I found He saw everything I did. He heard everything I heard. Though the work I did was unwitnessed by any other human besides the boys, it was seen and noted by the Ancient of Days.

As the new school year approached, we searched for a pediatric dentist who had experience with special needs children and called for an appointment. We were put on a waiting list. One day I got the call that an appointment was available and scheduled. I explained Matthew's needs to the scheduling nurse. She assured me the dentist could handle whatever challenges his needs presented.

I took Matthew to our initial appointment full of trepidation. Given his inability to follow a one-step direction, and his constant stimming behaviors, I could visualize him wreaking havoc on the dentist's exam room and instruments within moments. He could not sit in the dental exam chair without my hands-on help; the possibility of him remaining still and compliant was nearly impossible. I explained this to the scheduling nurse, the attending nurse, and the dentist to no avail. I knew once they saw how he reacted, they would understand. The dentist and nurse wanted to try him in the dental chair to see how he reacted, so I helped them lift him from his wheelchair into the dentist's chair. As I expected, his arms and legs flailed wildly, swiping at the neatly arranged dental instruments and lights. He twisted and flopped his body and flailed his arms and legs, spinning wildly in the dentist's chair until he was hanging sideways and head down in the dentist's chair. Unknowingly, his legs were poised to kick the tray of dental instruments, sending them airborne. I grabbed his legs in one fell swoop and scooped him out of the dentist's chair. The dentist and nurse stood gaping, slack-jawed and wide-eyed. They said nothing.

I calmed Matthew, squeezing him with firm deep pressure as I spoke to the dentist. I asked her if she could feasibly examine him in his wheelchair. She agreed to try. I lifted Matthew into his wheelchair, and secured him firmly, explaining to them that I would have to be hands-on, but would do my best to be helpful and stay out of their way. I would arrange his wheelchair as close to their instruments and lights as possible, and I would secure his hands if someone else could hold his head still. We gamed out our strategy, called in an extra nurse, and prepared for action. We had a narrow time window to work and gather data. We were all assembled and ready. The dentist gave the countdown and we all manned our posts. I crouched beside Matthew's wheelchair and secured his hands, Matthew squirmed and whimpered. I caught his eye and began to sing softly of heaven and Jesus's love. A nurse held Matthew's head still as the dentist placed the X-ray films, held his jaws closed and gave the signal to the radiology tech. It was done. The dentist did her exam and cleaning quickly. Matthew was crying and whimpering, his mouth forced wide open. I sang on, squinting away my own tears as I pressed my face against his legs. The dentist gave the "all clear," backed away, and exhaled. The nurses did the same. I maneuvered Matthew's wheelchair away from the equipment and instruments, speaking softly and calmly to him as we packed up to leave. Following that initial appointment, the dentist knew the dental chair was not an option for Matthew. She and her staff had learned the protocol with Matthew's appointments. Even though each appointment was a stress-filled ordeal, they were short-lived, which made them more doable.

As the winter semester began, it became increasingly clear that Matthew was in constant pain. After several visits and discussions with our primary doctors, we determined the source of his pain was most likely either his ears or teeth. Since Matthew was nonverbal and seemed to have a high pain tolerance, we had to make an educated guess. Though he had constant issues with ear infections and had ear tubes placed and replaced frequently, that didn't seem like the current issue. The pain source was most likely his teeth.

I called our pediatric dentist for an appointment; we were put on a waiting list. Matthew was not only in constant pain but was nearly choking with each meal as he would not chew his food. I began pureeing his food in the food processor to the consistency of oatmeal; he could eat without choking, but his pain continued. I did my best to manage his pain by layering over-the-counter pain medicine. When that no longer worked, we landed in the emergency room for stronger medication. On the prescription pain medicine, he was either stoned or knocked out; adjusting the dosages reduced side effects somewhat. When the appointment day arrived, the oral surgeon determined he likely needed full oral surgery. It was highly probable she would have to remove all of his molars, but she wouldn't know the extent of the damage and decay until she examined him under full sedation. She put us on her surgery waiting list indicating she would watch for the earliest opening in the surgery schedule. I began praying for an opening in the operating room schedule.

After several weeks of waiting, we had a surgery date. I followed our same evening regimen at home. I needed to drive separately as Matthew's was the first surgery of the morning. As usual, Matthew could not eat or drink before the surgery, so it was imperative that he not wake up before the time to leave. I quickly and quietly executed my perfectly timed plan; I loaded the bags and Mark carried Matthew to his car seat. Thankfully, he remained sound asleep. Mark stood in the driveway, waving as we left. Mark would join me in the same-day surgery waiting room after he took Luke to school.

We had been through the same-day surgery routine countless times and breezed through the security protocols and check-in. The wait time was minimal, as it was early morning. We were quickly received by a team of smiling nurses in brightly colored scrubs. Matthew slept through the prep and barely moved as the nurses began his IV sedation. A nurse gave me a smiling "thumbs-up" and I headed for the same-day surgery waiting room. It was a large open room arranged with chairs and tables in small groupings. Bright cartoonish trees were painted on the walls, and grinning monkeys and wide-eyed birds were peering through the branches. A receptionist sat behind a desk. I checked in as usual and settled in a darkened corner. I looked for the familiar coffee machine but found an upgraded version in its place. My weary brain halted at the many decisions involved: Cappuccino? Latte? Flavor Syrups? I opted for black. The rich aroma wafted upward; I inhaled deeply as the coffee sputtered into my paper cup. I returned to my darkened corner and waited. A morning news show played on a television mounted in the corner, and a sports program played on another.

My phone buzzed; Mark was in the parking garage and was headed my way. After several moments he joined me. I pointed out the coffee machine and the sports program on the television across the room. "So?" Mark asked. I relayed that Matthew's check-in, wait time, and sedation had been uneventful and that the receptionist would let us know that the oral surgeon was ready to brief us on the surgery. I explained that she would talk to us in one of the conference rooms. Mark got a coffee from the machine, opting for a cappuccino, and settled in for the long wait.

I rested my head against the wall and talked to my Father in Heaven. "Lord, we've been here many times, but this is different. This is a game-changer for Matthew. He'll never eat solid food again if they pull all his molars. Lord, guide the surgeon even now. Give her wisdom and guide her hands and instruments." I alternately prayed and watched the local news show.

"Parents for Matthew?" the receptionist called. I waved and made eye contact; she pointed to one of the nearby conference rooms. The oral surgeon came in wearing blue scrubs and a hat. "Matthew did well," she said, "we did have to remove all his molars and place silver ones. All his food will have to be pureed from now on. He will not be able to eat solid food at all." She paused, eyeing Mark and me for our reaction. I nodded; it was as I expected and as I feared. She confirmed that the level of wear from grinding and decay was most likely his pain source. The source of that pain was eliminated; once his mouth healed, all should be well. Eliminating his pain was a massive relief. Pureeing his food added another step to my overwhelming workload, but it was doable.

Matthew was still in recovery, she said. They would call us when he was ready to go home. We resumed our waiting in our darkened corner. Soon, the receptionist gave us the "thumbs up" and we retraced our steps into the elevator and down the long hallway to surgery. Matthew lay on a gurney. He was drowsy but waking up. The nurse handed me a clipboard with discharge papers, Lines for my signature were highlighted in yellow. I scribbled my signature and nodded, as she gave discharge instructions. Mark helped me dress Matthew and carried him to his car seat. Matthew was still sleeping when I pulled into our driveway; Mark pulled in next to me, carried Matthew into the house, and laid him on his bed. Matthew sighed deeply and rolled over.

The source of Matthew's constant pain was eliminated, but things were different now. In some ways, it was a small step downward; in others, it was a massive step downward. Life had changed again, but I trusted my Lord was in control no matter what changes, whether large or small, lay ahead. We were home but in a completely different place.

FOOD FOR THOUGHT:

1. Are you in a season marked by hard circumstances? What is God asking of you in this difficult season? How could "Do the next thing" be a helpful concept during this season of difficulty?

2. Personal experience and His Word is what fueled my trust in Him. How are Scripture and your personal experiences with God fueling your trust in Him these days? How is He speaking to you through His Word? How could trusting Him, even in seasons of obscurity and menial work, also make this season a sweet resting place with Him?

CHAPTER 7

MY EVER-PRESENT HELP IN BRUTAL REALITIES

"God is our refuge and strength, a very present help in trouble."

Psalm 46:1, ESV

"...fear not, for I am with you; be not dismayed, for I am your God; I will strengthen you, I will help you, I will uphold you with my righteous right hand."

Isaiah 41:10, ESV

Scriptures that speak of God's deliverance can sound like empty platitudes in the face of harsh realities. They can sound like "pie in the sky," offering little to those of us living life in the trenches, who carry on battle-weary, and for whom reality is an "in your face" reminder of unanswered prayers. What bridges the gap between the brutal realities we face and truth upheld in Scripture? I found it was trust in God.

I worked hard to soldier on, stalwartly grounded in truth

though harsh realities surrounded me. My days were governed by work, Matthew's bus time, medication schedule, and our evening routine. Because Matthew had Lennox Gastaut, he had several seizures each day. I kept a running log of their times, duration, and type at our neurologist's request. Seizures that lasted over six minutes, or ones that wouldn't stop with Diastat, required a phone call. The notebook that served as my seizure logbook stayed on the kitchen table. Matthew's needs made each day painful. Seizures and sadness were woven into the fabric of my life.

As I sat with Matthew through his seizures and struggles, I continued to sing hymns for us both, as I'd been doing since before he and Luke were born. As I sang, "*Through many dangers, toils and snares, I have already come . . .*", those "dangers, toils and snares" were now associated with certain emergency room visits, hospital rooms and long nights. As I softly crooned "*. . . His grace has brought us safe thus far, and grace will lead me home!*" I knew it was true, because He had carried us our entire journey, and He was carrying us now.

When I first began this desert journey years ago, I found God to be completely trustworthy. He still was. However, the circumstances were more intense now, and the stakes were much higher should I falter. Stepping forward in audacious faith still felt like stepping onto a single steel cable suspended over a yawning canyon. That proverbial steel cable now stretched across different canyons. Yet, He and I had a track record together now. He had sustained me and rewarded my obedience with more of Himself at every turn. I knew His voice. I knew His heart in ways I could never have known before. I knew this One with whom I dwelt in this barren place was the Yahweh of Sinai, Who spoke with Moses as Friend with friend. This One who held my boys and me was The God of Angel Armies. I also found The God of Angel Armies was also The

Lover of My Soul. When I knew the One Who called me forward in trusting obedience was the One who formed Earth, knows each star by name, and yet drew me into tender friendship, it stunned and quieted my soul. Whatever He asked of me was for my good and His glory, so how could I refuse? I found myself saying: "I will do what You ask of me, for the rest of my life, and will leave the outcome to You." It was poignantly apparent each day that Jesus was all I had. As in earlier days, He was all I needed.

Trusting God didn't negate the realities before me, but it drew me into an intimate friendship with the Most High. Within that intimacy, truth soaked deep into my soul, revealing that truth trumps our earthly reality. Reality surrounded me, but truth buoyed me in the choppy sea of painful circumstances. The same truths that had introduced themselves in earlier days now became my close friends. I clung to the truth of Scripture as my lifeline to keep me from drowning in the sea of painful circumstances, and each day was simply a walk of faithful obedience. However, each time I acted in faithful obedience, I laid another strand of steel cable to my faith bridge. Day by day, with each act of obedience, with each portion of Scripture memorized, sermon ingested, each tearful, pleading prayer, each hymn sung in the darkness, the more the strong cables in my faith bridge became tightly interwoven. These practices strengthened both me and my faith bridge. In turn, the bridge supported me to fight on as I continued living my life suspended over mist-enshrouded canyons, walking upon the bridge of faith and guided by my Savior's unseen hand.

The practices and mindsets I learned in earlier days now sustained me in the barren place. However, I could not rest upon my laurels. For the boys' and my survival, I had to become more unflinching in the face of our increasingly difficult circumstances. I had to mine more gems from Scripture, adding more truth to my arsenal. Sun-drenched morning devotions in an overstuffed arm-chair had become impossible long ago, but a steady intake of truth was vital for my survival. The same teaching ministry on Christian radio that sustained me in earlier days was vital now. I turned it on when I got up, and was making coffee and breakfast, and I turned it off as I switched off lights and locked doors at night. Truth flowed into my kitchen in a steady stream and I soaked my weary soul in its healing waters. The pastors who had taught me in earlier days became companions in my desert life. I listened as I washed dishes, cooked, and scrubbed floors. The constant flow of truth undergirded my faltering soul, and gave me the courage to step out in obedience, acting in faith upon Who He is.

I thought often of Moses's desert life. However, my attention turned toward those in-between years–year two through thirty-nine of his desert life. In those in-between years, Moses's life was filled with sheepherding and family concerns. Egypt's splendor was long ago and far away. Calling down plagues and leading the exodus were tasks for another day. These were the appointed days of desert life, learning obedience and faithfulness among drudgery and the simple dailiness of life. That is where I dwelt.

When I submitted to the place and circumstances God had assigned me, I found both a settled sadness and a settled peace. There was sadness because Matthew's struggles remained despite my fervent prayers. Despite the sadness, there was a quiet peace as well. I knew I had prayed faithfully. I knew I was doing everything I could in His strength. For reasons all His own, this was His place for us now. It was my job to learn the lessons one could only learn in this desert place.

Despite my enormous dreams for a writing, teaching, and speaking ministry, none of that was His will for me now. It was His will that I do the simple, tedious tasks daily set before me. No one expected me to write a book, launch a website, or give a speech. However, He did expect that whether I was scrubbing the bathroom floor, cleaning up disgusting messes, or persevering in the taxing caregiving demands with kindness and diligence, that it was all done as a pleasing sacrifice for my audience of One.

Often all I could see was Matthew's struggle and my sadness, but God was about something greater. At times, all I wanted was to fast-forward through the pain but to do so meant that I was missing something valuable. Diamonds are formed by long, slow pressure and intense heat. God was purifying me in the intense heat and pressure. Though intense heat and pressure are unpleasant, Jesus promised His presence within the fire, just as He did with the three Hebrews in the fiery furnace. When I tried to fast-forward through the fire, I missed the glory of His presence beside me in flames. I determined it was worth the intensity of the flames to know the glory of His presence beside me in the fire.

In the daily grind of caregiving, God was speaking. As He'd done before, He dropped an image upon me. He showed me where we were headed. Late one night, I was in the shower. I often prayed and cried in the shower as even the ugliest cry could be washed down the drain. I turned off the water and grasped the door handle as He dropped an image that left me breathless. In the image, He took me by the shoulders and walked me to the front of a chapel. In the front was a casket. I knew it was Matthew's without looking, and backed away in breathless horror, pressing my face into His chest. He held me there. "No Lord, really?" I whispered aloud in the shower. His fixed, piercing gaze told me all I needed to know. He held me as I wept both in the image and the shower. He'd told me where we were heading, yet I didn't know the timing. I knew He would be with me holding me no matter how the days ahead unfolded.

Though Matthew was often ill, and frequently hospitalized, he'd never been so seriously ill that his life was in question. That changed with his first bout of pneumonia. Matthew was struggling through another of his ear infections and respiratory illnesses; I did my best to ease his discomfort and care for his needs. Sometimes he slept deeply when ill, and other times he could not. This time he could not. I followed our evening routine, hoping a warm shower would work its magic—thankfully, it did. I settled Matthew in bed. "Lord please let him go to sleep," I prayed as I headed for the pile of dried-on dishes in the kitchen sink. My reflection stared back from the kitchen window—what remained of a ponytail drooped sideways, and cavernous shadows swallowed my eyes. Warm water swished into the sink as I squirted blue dish soap into the stream; the bubbles rose in a shimmering mound, iridescent in the dim light. I squished the mound of bubbles in my hand, and plunged my hands into the warm water, lingering in its warmth.

I worked as quickly and quietly as possible lest the slightest clatter disturbed Matthew. Then I heard it: his swooshing noise. He was awake. My heart sank. Hurriedly, I scrubbed the remaining dishes, stacking them into the dishwasher. He began knocking on the walls and rattling the baby gate. He grasped for me as I opened the gate and I scooped him onto my lap—he was feverish. I hurried to the cabinet for the thermometer and a syringe of orange sticky medicine; his fever was 102. I showed him the syringe, and he smiled in recognition and sipped it as I slowly squirted it in his mouth. Once again, I scooped him into my lap and began to sing.

"The Lord is my shepherd. I'll walk with Him always. He leads by still waters. I'll walk with Him always," I sang. I pressed my cheek against his head, his hair was soft bristles against my skin. I sang on, rocking him in my lap, singing as I prayed: "Gentle Shepherd, lead me now. Give me wisdom for the challenges of this night.

Give me the strength and grace this night requires." As I sang on, Matthew slumped heavily against me, his breathing became deep and rhythmic. He was asleep, yet I dared not move him. A holy stillness hung about the room, urging me to stay. I rested against the wall, soaking in the stillness, as I prayed on, tears slipping silently down. I eased Matthew onto his bed and prepared to slip away—feeling his forehead as I left—less warm. "The medicine is taking hold. He'll sleep soundly now. Tomorrow will be a fresh, new day," I thought. "After this, I'll have some supper," I mused as I cleaned the kitchen. I heard him again: swooshing, knocking, and rattling his baby gate.

He was still warm; his eyes were wild as he began his characteristic spinning. He spied the open gate lurching down the hallway into the living room. I clamored after him. He flopped and rolled against the loveseat, then the sofa, darting from one end of the room to the other—wide-eyed. I scooped him into my lap once again, he wriggled away, darting back and forth, eyes wild. I grabbed my phone and called the on-call nurse in the ER. I had to leave a message. I heard the buzz of the garage door; Mark was home from work. He stopped in the hallway, lunchbox in hand, as Matthew darted past him wide-eyed. Mark shot me a questioning glance; I did my best to explain. Mark set my purse, shoes, and hospital bag in the hallway and disappeared into the bedroom. He knew the drill by this time.

I sat on the sofa, waiting for the on-call nurse to return my call, watching intently as Matthew darted up and down, and prayed. "Lord, give me wisdom. What is wrong? You know what's wrong and how to help him. Please show me." I prayed on: "Lord, he seems terrified." I said aloud, "Show me what to do." I watched Matthew intently. The nurse returned my call; she said a doctor would call me soon. I hung up and waited, weighing my options—

should I call the ambulance or take him to the emergency room myself? As I watched, Matthew's behavior changed within moments. He stopped darting momentarily and backed into a corner gasping, his mouth wide open. "He can't breathe, Lord!" I said aloud. "Pneumonia! He's got pneumonia!" I jammed my feet into my shoes and flung my purse and hospital bag over my shoulder. I scooped up Matthew, grabbed my keys, and was out the door. This could not wait; he needed a doctor now. I buckled Matthew into his car seat, grabbed my phone, and called the emergency room phone nurse once again. The answering machine message began. I pulled out, barreling through the empty streets and onto the interstate, watching Matthew in the rearview mirror. "Mama's helping you, Baby. Mama's getting you help!" I said to him. "It's gonna be okay." I zipped through the deserted downtown and swung into a parking space under a security light. There was a hospital transport wagon wedged against its base.

Grabbing the wagon, I lifted him into it, clicking the van lock as I pulled Matthew toward the lighted Emergency Room entrance. My phone buzzed in my hand; it was the on-call nurse. "Yes ma'am, we're walking up to the ER entrance now," I said. "Good, I'll meet you there," she said and hung up. The emergency room doors whooshed open. A security guard in a crisp white shirt sat behind a podium, his name badge said Martin. "May I see your ID?" he asked.

A blonde woman rounded the corner behind him. "You must be Paula," she said. I nodded. She waved me through, assuring Martin I was safe and led us around the corner to an exam room directly across from the nurse's station. She clipped an O2 monitor on Matthew's finger as we lifted him onto the bed. It said 88. She smiled, "I'm going to start some oxygen and see how he does," she said, adjusting a nearby hose and holding the cannula under his nose. "I'll hold it," I offered. I needed to be close in case his agitation returned. Nurses came and went, checking his oxygen levels. Matthew lay still, breathing. His oxygen levels inched upward—89, 92, 97. He was calming; he could breathe now.

A doctor came, examining him as she questioned me about my concerns. "I'm not a doctor, but I wonder if he's got pneumonia," I said. I highlighted the events of the past few hours. She nodded, listening to me as she examined him. She assured me that Matthew was in good hands, spoke quietly to the nurse, and they both left. Matthew was drifting off to sleep. I stood beside his gurney holding the oxygen cannula under his nose—I too, simply breathed. Matthew was asleep. I dragged a chair beside Matthew's gurney. The television in the corner played 1970's sitcoms: *Barney Miller* was on deck.

The nurse returned and removed Matthew's oxygen. "We'll see how he does without it, and maybe send you home tonight," she said. "You have oxygen at home, right?"

"No, I don't," I said flatly. Tightness gripped my gut. 'They cannot send us home—not now.', I thought. I said nothing.

"Oh, that makes a difference," she said and was gone. She returned with orders for bloodwork and chest x-ray and checked Matthew's oxygen. It was dropping again. The nurse set the cannula back under his nose, looping it over his ears.

Martin, the security guard tapped on the glass door of the unit and asked for my ID. I nodded; I knew the drill. Martin returned within moments with my ID, and the adhesive security badge I'd worn countless times. I peeled it and slapped it onto the front of my ugly brown hoodie, it was upside down and crooked; I didn't care. Matthew's hand rested limply against the sheet; I slipped my hand under his. Hot tears stung my eyes as I rested my forehead on the edge of the gurney. My tears dripped onto the sheet as I prayed, "Lord, You know what's best. Please don't let them send Matthew home prematurely. Get us the help we need, Lord. Matthew needs help, don't let them neglect him," I prayed. I felt my forehead sinking into the mattress as I prayed. The beeping monitors sounded far away, I felt myself sinking into sleep but was powerless against its pull. Soft footsteps, then rustling papers roused me. It was the nurse. She was checking his oxygen levels; she gently poked around the inside of his elbow for a good vein. The lab techs were on their way down, she said. I nodded numbly; I knew how Matthew's blood draws usually went, and I knew my role in the process.

Lab techs peered into our unit, scanning the code on the patient ID bracelet looped around Matthew's ankle. The nurse directed the techs to the good veins she located. Weighing their options, they gently tapped on veins in his wrists, arms, and feet. They opted for his arm. Matthew awoke, thrashing in confusion. I caught his eye. "It's okay, Baby," I said gently, "Mama's here. Mama's here." I laid my body over his and began to sing of heaven and Jesus's love.

I rested my head on his chest as the tech tapped the vein, then snapped the blue tourniquet. She positioned the needle, poised for the stick. She eyed me, and asked, "We good, Mom?" I nodded. "3, 2, 1, and, stick!" Matthew whimpered and grimaced; the techs exhaled. Matthew's blood flowed into the test vials, and techs deftly handed empty and full vials to one another, labeling them as they worked. The techs positioned and taped a narrow green board under Matthew's arm, fixing it in an extended position. Our nurse returned, starting IV fluids. Once again, I rested my forehead on the edge of Matthew's gurney. The chatter and canned laughter drifted down from the TV. I closed my eyes, praying as I waited.

"Lord, You see us here in this ER unit. Oh God Who sees, see us here! Help Matthew breathe. Don't let our needs be overlooked or passed over," I prayed.

"Chest X-ray for Matthew?" A radiologist peered into our unit. I nodded. He rolled a massive machine beside Matthew's gurney. Several nurses appeared, as if from thin air. They repositioned Matthew on the gurney. A metal arm extended and the X-ray plates positioned. The tech handed out heavy black aprons, "Any chance you ladies may be pregnant?" he asked. A gray-haired nurse laughed. He counted down and took the image, repeating it on Matthew's back. The ordeal was over as quickly as it had begun. Our nurse placed the cannula back under his nose, watching him intently. She stood facing our unit as she charted. The intro music to *Three's Company* began on the TV; I resumed my waiting position. Matthew was sleeping. A pin-point of pain throbbed behind my right eye; my stomach growled. "Supper?" I thought. "I never ate supper. Lunch? Surely I ate lunch." My stomach disagreed.

The doctor returned, wheeling up a stool to chat. "X-rays show pneumonia in both lobes," she said. "Matthew is not maintaining oxygen levels on his own. We think he needs to be admitted." I exhaled and nodded. "We'll start IV antibiotics and get you upstairs to a room as soon as possible," she said and was gone. "Thank you, Lord," I breathed.

I resumed my waiting position. "Can I get you anything?" It was our nurse once again. "Water? Have you eaten anything?" she asked. I shook my head. "I'll see what I have," she said. She returned with a kid-sized water bottle and a Lunchable. "It's all I have right now, but the kitchen opens at 6 AM," she smiled apologetically. I took it gratefully and glanced at the TV—*Lavern and Shirley*. It was nearly 4 AM. "I can text Mark an update by 5:30. He will also need instructions on getting Luke around and off to school," I mused. The absurd antics and canned laughter from the TV squawked on. I waited and prayed.

"Lord, we've been in this ER many times, but he's never had pneumonia. This is very different. Please help us," I prayed.

"Is that fresh coffee?" Our nurse asked a young man in a food service uniform. He was wheeling a cart bearing a gleaming pot. Our nurse caught my eye and pointed questioningly at the pot. I nodded. "How we doin'?" she asked cheerfully, handing me a Styrofoam cup of steaming coffee. "I thought you could use this too," she said, handing me a cream cheese Danish in a cellophane wrapper. She checked Matthew's oxygen levels and made some adjustments, then she scooted up the leg of Matthew's pajama pants, gently poking his legs. I watched her intently; her face told me nothing. As she left, I did as she had done. I saw nothing unusual. I stood fingering the blue fleece of his pajama pants. "Lord?" I questioned, "What's happening? What is she looking for?" A heaviness settled in my gut.

She quickly returned saying our room was ready; a transport team was en route. I texted Mark. He was up; I opted for a phone call. "He's got pneumonia so we're being admitted. I'll text you the room number in a minute." I said. The transport team arrived. They worked quickly; we were on the move. Matthew barely stirred. I leaned against the elevator wall listening to its hum as we hurtled upward. Matthew stirred and caught my eye. "It's okay, Baby, mama's here," I said to him, and he closed his eyes. The elevator stopped; the transport team wheeled the hospital bed past the nurses' station and into a room I immediately recognized. I texted Mark our room number. A nurse handed me his blue fleece pajama pants and shirt; he was now in a hospital gown.

A doctor came. "Hi, you must be mom," she smiled reassuringly as she examined Matthew. Nurses in brightly colored scrubs bustled in and out of Matthew's room; just as quickly, the room emptied except for one nurse. She watched Matthew intently; she changed the oxygen cannula for a mask. She pulled back Matthew's sheet, pressing her finger into his leg as I'd seen the ER nurse do. "Everything okay?" I asked.

"He's not maintaining his oxygen levels as I'd like," she said. "We'll try the mask and see if that helps. I'm watching him on my monitor." She said, pointing to the computer screen on her desk right outside Matthew's door. She slipped away. I slipped to his bedside. His oxygen level read 86. Our nurse returned, I pointed at the read-out, and she nodded. "I'm calling the doctor back," she said. She moved the sheet and poked his leg again. Her finger left a whitish imprint. There was gray-blue mottling around his feet and ankles. Tightness rose in my gut. The doctor arrived, eyeing Matthew's oxygen levels and poking his legs. He talked quickly and quietly to the nurse with furrowed brows, she went to her desk and made a call. She returned and stood beside me. "Matthew is declining rapidly. He's going into septic shock," she said. "We're moving him directly to PICU, with your permission." I nodded, stunned. "We've called the transport team," she said and was gone.

The doctor left and I rushed to Matthew's bedside. I sucked in my breath as hot tears stung my eyes. I pressed my cheek against his head, my tears slipped into his hair and onto his forehead. I pursed my lips together tightly, stifling the sobs threatening to burst forth. My mind flashed to the chapel scene God had shown me weeks ago. "Now Lord? Today? You mean now?" I asked. I forced myself to breathe slowly and deeply.

The hospital intercom broke in, "Immediate medical emergency. Repeating, immediate medical emergency." They gave the floor and room number—it was Matthew's room number. I froze. "He's dying—right now, today, he's dying!" I whispered to myself.

The same transport team arrived. One nurse talked on a two-way radio. They tended to Matthew beside the doctor and nurse. I backed out of the way. A young man in a crisp white lab coat approached. "I'm the pharmacist," he said, "just a few questions about meds." Medication names, dosages, and times spewed from me, I prayed I was right. As the pharmacist left, I saw Mark waiting across the hallway. He cast me a questioning glance; I waved him in. "They're moving him to PICU, he's not doing well," I said.

The transport team was on the move. "Let's go," I said to Mark. We scrambled after the transport team, squeezing into the same elevator. No one spoke as we descended. The elevator bumped to a stop and slid open. The nurses maneuvered Matthew's bed into a broad beige hallway and morning light streamed from a bay of tall windows. Double doors swung open as we approached; a PICU nurse waited beside a glassed-in unit. Mark and I stood silently outside. The transport team spoke quietly with the nurse and were gone. A doctor arrived, examining Matthew as he conferred with the nurse. The nurse approached us. "Would you be more comfortable in the waiting room?" she asked. "We'll settle him and then come get you." I nodded.

She swiped her badge, and a series of double doors opened. She waved us toward the waiting room. Mark and I stood awkwardly in the center of the waiting room, people staring. Grasping my arm, Mark steered me toward a darkened corner. I plopped down my purse and sank into a chair. Mark sat beside me, "So...?" he questioned, "What's going on?"

I sighed deeply, "He has pneumonia. He's in septic shock. He's not doing well, which is why he's in PICU," I said flatly.

"Not doing well? What do you mean? Like...?" his voice trailed off. I nodded, and my tears slid downward, dripping from my chin. I swiped them away with my sleeve, leaned my head back against the wall, and closed my eyes. Tears slid into my ears and down my neck.

"He'll get better, right? Right?" Mark questioned. I opened my eyes; he was staring at me. The rush of questions begging for answers flashed across his face; he just stared at me, shaking his head. "No!".

"I hope so, but don't know," I answered. "He's in the right place now. We hope and pray for the best." We sat in silence.

"Matthew's parents?" It was the receptionist. She swiped her badge and pointed us back through the double doors. Matthew lay motionless, an oxygen mask nearly swallowing his face. I lifted the sheet. Each of Matthew's legs was encased in what looked like a massive blood pressure cuff. It puffed and whooshed as I watched. "They're compression devices," the nurse said, "to keep him from getting blood clots." I nodded.

"How was Luke?" I asked Mark. "What did you tell him?"

"He was fine. I just said Matthew was back in hospital," he said. "He was concerned, but he's used to it, I think."

"He's used to it," I mused. "He's used to his brother being in the hospital."

We stood at Matthew's bedside in silence. Mark still held my hospital bag. "What now?" he asked. I shrugged, "I am here, so I guess you're at home with Luke," I said.

"I'll call into work then," he said.

"Sorry, I don't know what else to do," I said. We stood in awkward silence.

"Have you been up all night?" he asked. I nodded. "If I go, maybe you can sleep." He nodded toward the green vinyl recliner behind me. I nodded, and he stowed my hospital bag beside the chair.

"I'll walk you down to the parking garage," I said. "These hallways can be a maze." Mark agreed. "I'll be back in a minute," I told the nurse. She nodded.

Mark's gaze rested on Matthew. "Poor little guy," he said sadly. We turned to go.

The double doors swung open as we approached. I led Mark through a maze of doors and hallways to the elevator bay. "I can make it from here," he said, "Go try and get some rest." I nodded. An elevator door opened behind him; he stepped inside, waved, and was gone.

I returned to Matthew's unit, as there was nothing else to do. My mind ran wildly through the scenarios the evening may present; I jerked my mind back from its rampage. I sank into the green recliner and stared at the reality before me; the reality stared back. Matthew's long, dark lashes lay in stark contrast against his pale cheeks. The cuffs puffed and whooshed on his legs. Bags of IV fluids and antibiotics hung from the IV pole nearby, flowing down a trail of tubing through the ports in his arm. His right arm lay stiffly extended, taped to the same green board the lab techs placed during the night. There was nothing to do but sit, so I sat. I let my eyes close as the whooshing and beeping faded around me.

High-pitched beeping startled me awake. The nurse was changing Matthew's IV bag. She suggested I reserve an overnight room at the Ronald McDonald parent facility, as they were on a first come, first served basis. She pointed down the beige hallway with the tall curved windows. The familiar sign marked the doorway. I made my request and filled out the registration card. A volunteer took me to my room, pointing out the shower room on the way. The room was simply furnished with a bed, lamp, and nightstand. The bed lured me toward a nap, but I needed to be near

Matthew. In Matthew's unit, I sank into the green recliner; there was nothing else to do.

Our nurse pointed me toward the parents' quiet room. I wandered in that direction and found a room with a few recliners, a large-screen television, and a kitchenette. Tucked into an alcove sat a small desk with a computer. I made coffee and sat down to write an update for family and church friends. A heavy knot tightened in my chest as I began writing out the events that landed us here. Though I'd experienced them, writing them out solidified them. Matthew had nearly died. He was still in danger, but in the right place to receive appropriate care. I finished my update, edited it, and clicked send. As I re-read my email, it sounded oddly similar to the medical updates I'd received from parents in similar situations. Their emails were full of medical terminology, hard realities, and simple requests for prayer. Mine sounded the same; I was one of them.

At suppertime, I found a foil pan in the fridge in the Ronald McDonald's parent facility laden with spaghetti casserole. A date was neatly written on the lid beside a sticker marking it as a gift from the women's auxiliary from a nearby church. I located a plate and utensils and poked the casserole into the microwave. I had no desire to eat but knew I had to. I stabbed the pasta and placed it in my mouth; it lay there like an immovable mass. I forced myself to chew and swallow; I managed a few bites. I swiped the remaining casserole into the trash, with an apology and a "thank you" to the women's auxiliary. I returned to the green recliner and tried to pray; wordless groaning was all that rose from my soul.

A dark-haired nurse urged me towards the comfort of my reserved room, assuring me they would contact me if anything changed. I reluctantly agreed and made the trek down the beige hallway once again. As I clicked the door closed, I noticed a full-length mirror mounted on the back of the door. The remains of a ponytail still hung limply; the cavernous shadows swallowing my eyes were deeper. The ugly brown hoodie enveloped me and my ID sticker remained upside down and sideways where I'd stuck it during the night. I found a pair of pajamas in my hospital bag and headed for the shower room. No matter how stressful a day, a shower provided the opportunity for a reset. I could cry and pray in the shower and start fresh. I relished the possibility of a good cry. I stood in the warm water letting the day wash away, and began to pray. The tears flowed as I prayed, choking sobs seized me, forcing me to the shower floor; warm water pounded my back as I sank on all fours. I was trembling as rasping screams burst out of me. I rolled into a fetal position on the shower floor and let the warm water wash over me. I finished my shower, returned to my room, and lay on the bed for a long time. I searched the nightstand for the Gideon Bible, finding the familiar psalms. Focus evaded me, so I began the conversation I'd been trying to have since this ordeal began.

"Lord? What just happened? Pneumonia? Matthew nearly died today! You weren't kidding—the chapel? We're in uncharted waters!" I prayed. There was only silence. I slipped into bed and let my inarticulate groaning rise to His ears. As I did so, His promises wafted over me: *". . .fear not, for I am with you; be not dismayed, for I am your God; I will strengthen you, I will help you, I will uphold you with my righteous right hand." Isaiah 41:10, ESV*

He'd been my Stronghold our entire journey, and He would be now. The road ahead would be rocky and uphill; He had promised as much. However, rocky and uphill roads are where He is most hands-on. He'd proven himself faithful a thousand times over; He would still. *"The eternal God is your dwelling place, and underneath are the everlasting arms..."(Deuteronomy 33:2, ESV)*. My boys and

I rested in the everlasting arms of The Ancient of Days! He was strong enough to handle whatever lay ahead.

The next morning, I began what I referred to as my PICU routine. I dressed and trekked down the beige hallway to Matthew's PICU unit. I got updates from the nurses, called Luke with an update and morning chat, made a coffee in the parents' room, and journaled and read my Bible as I waited for the doctor. Concern and prayers poured into my inbox following my email update; they warmed and comforted my battle-weary soul. Days flowed into a week, and Matthew was improving; he was moved to a room on a regular nursing floor. Within days on the regular nursing floor, Matthew had stabilized and we were released. Matthew seemed relieved to be home. He seemed to know something major had just gone down; I did as well.

FOOD FOR THOUGHT:

1. Does the truth sound like "pie in the sky" as you face brutal realities? What harsh realities have put you in the trenches? Trust in God is a powerful link to peace despite our harsh realities. Does that concept seem lofty? How have you experienced the peace of God while facing brutal realities? What role has Scripture played in that process?

2. What is the relationship between trust and peace? What role does Scripture play in that relationship? Read Isaiah 26:3. What link does this Scripture make between trust in God and peace? Is the idea of trusting God a difficult leap for you? How have you trusted God in the past? Has he proved himself trustworthy? What were the circumstances? How did He show Himself as trustworthy?

CHAPTER 8

ETERNAL GLORY
ON THE LONG HAUL

"For this light momentary affliction is preparing for us an eternal weight of glory beyond all comparison, as we look not to the things that are seen but to the things that are unseen. For the things that are seen are transient, but the things that are unseen are eternal."

2 Corinthians 4:17-18, ESV

"And I heard a loud voice from the throne saying, "Behold, the dwelling place of God is with man. He will dwell with them, and they will be his people, and God himself will be with them as their God. He will wipe away every tear from their eyes, and death shall be no more, neither shall there be mourning, nor crying, nor pain anymore, for the former things have passed away."

Revelation 21:3-4, ESV

As the school year ended in 2010, the kindergarten teacher in the classroom where I was assigned suggested that I seek a transfer to the early childhood building within our district. At that building, there was a four-day workweek for para-professionals and they would accommodate my half-day status. I made the inquiry and filled out the transfer paperwork, and it was done. I would start in my third building in the fall.

Luke continued to kick off his summers with a trip to church family camp at the lake. My friend Cynthia and her family adopted Luke for the weekend, and he was part of the mix of the other kids and families from our church community group. As always, he returned sun-bronzed, hungry, and tightly wound from three days of little sleep and non-stop activity.

Since Luke was a preschooler, he'd been asking for a dog. I always punted that discussion to Mark as I was overwhelmed with Matthew's care, and certainly didn't need more work and commotion in my world. Mark always told him that he could get a dog when he turned eleven or when we were in a different house.

In the spring of 2010, Mark began the search for a suitable dog. He quietly perused pet adoption sites and sent me photos of different options. Because of Matthew's special needs, certain breeds and sizes were out of the question. We needed a large dog that couldn't be crushed or injured if Matthew fell on it. We needed a dog with a gentle and patient temperament that could appropriately respond with understanding and compassion for Matthew's needs. We needed the right dog, not just any dog.

I was making copies in the teacher's workroom when Mark texted me a picture: a large golden lab-mix smiled up at me. He needed rescue from a high-kill shelter; he had been in several shelters and just needed a family. The shelter worker assured Mark that this dog had the patient, gentle temperament that we needed. He was temporarily fostering with a family, but their medical needs made the situation urgent. I texted Mark back, and we decided to proceed with the process. Mark made the calls and exchanged texts with the shelter worker; they scheduled an in-home visit to determine whether our home and yard were suitable for a large pet and whether we were a suitable family for such a responsibility. The home visit was scheduled for the upcoming weekend. I had one day to prepare.

Mark was home that afternoon, waiting for Luke to come home from school. Luke arrived home, flinging his backpack on his bedroom floor and perusing the kitchen for after-school snacks, as usual. "Luke, come here," Mark said as he swiped his phone, pulling up the photo of the large golden lab-mix. "I have something to show you."

Luke wandered in munching his cheese crackers. Mark held up his phone and showed Luke the picture of the large yellow lab. Luke stopped chewing and grabbed Mark's phone, staring at the image on the screen. "Are we getting a dog?" he asked, looking from the phone screen to Mark's face. Disbelief and guarded excitement danced across his face.

"We're working on it, Buddy," Mark said. "The lady from the pet adoption service is coming on Saturday to meet with us. She wants to be sure we have a fenced yard and that we'll be responsible pet owners."

Mark brought out his computer, and he and Luke sat together on the couch clicking through the photos and reading all the information about the large golden lab—his name was JoJo.

I waited for Matthew's bus beside the open front door and watched them. Mark read and re-read the information with Luke, quietly talking about the responsibilities of feeding, walking, and cleaning up after a dog.

"I'll walk him every day! I'll feed him and take care of him!"

Luke affirmed in wide-eyed agreement.

I spotted Matthew's yellow-orange bus rounding the corner and walked down the driveway to meet it as it rolled to a stop. As usual, the bus aid swung his backpack down the steps and walked Matthew down the steps to me. His safety harness remained looped around his shoulders and legs as he and I walked up the driveway. He stopped, grasping for me as we approached the front steps—his wordless request that I carry him.

"Why not?" I said to myself, as I hefted him onto my hip and lugged him up the steps and into the house. Mark and Luke were still on the couch clicking through the dog pictures, talking, and reading about him.

As I lifted Matthew into his feeding chair for his after-school snack, I glanced about at the clutter and disarray that followed my typical workweek and two boys with widely differing needs. I unpacked Matthew's backpack, stowing his bus safety harness in its usual place. I fixed Matthew's usual snack of graham crackers and milk, pulled up a kitchen chair, and sat down to feed him. Our suppertime conversation was dominated by talk of the new dog—where he would sleep, who would go with Luke to walk the new dog, and who may be his favorite person.

"I will need some help whipping this house into shape for this in-home visit," I said to Mark. He glanced about and agreed. We laid out a game plan and a timeline for after the boys were in bed. I hoped Matthew would fall asleep. He did. With the boys in bed, we got to work. Mark decluttered and dusted as I scrubbed and mopped the kitchen and bathrooms. We saved the vacuuming for the morning. The following morning, Mark received a text from the lady at the pet adoption service indicating the fostering family needed to move the process along due to their own medical concerns. It was all going to happen in one visit; we were getting a dog today. They would arrive by 2 pm.

Luke was over the moon with excitement. He rushed through breakfast, eager to run across the street to tell his friends about the new dog. Luke chattered incessantly, leaping about the house and asking to see the pictures on Mark's phone again and again. Mark ran the vacuum cleaner as I cared for Matthew as usual. His needs continued unabated despite the excitement surrounding the new dog.

Matthew watched Luke leap about with a questioning look. "Yes, Matthew, Luke is excited about getting a dog," I explained, unsure if he understood, but assuming he could do it on some level. "We're getting a dog today, Matthew. What do you think about that? Look at Luke! What is he doing?" Matthew's gaze flitted from Luke to my face; a faint smile played at his lips.

I thought through the many sources of potential agitation likely to arise throughout the afternoon. There would be three strangers and a dog in our home. Mark would need to be able to speak with the pet adoption lady and sign papers. We needed to assure the fostering family that JoJo was in good hands. I laid out a game plan in my mind as I worked through Matthew's regular med and feeding routine and made plans for lunch. As I cleared away the lunch dishes, I relayed to Mark the game plan I'd been orchestrating in my head all morning. We should invite the pet adoption lady and fostering family to bring JoJo into the house and get them settled. We should allow Luke's excitement to simmer down to a low boil, and then introduce Matthew into the mix. This meant that Matthew would have to stay in his room behind the baby gate until the initial commotion passed. Mark agreed it was a decent plan, although not perfect. Matthew inadvertently cooperated beautifully; he flopped on his bed and was soon sound asleep. It was great for the moment, but I knew he would wake up once the excitement began—and rightly so. Matthew was part of our family. He should be part of the meeting and welcoming our new dog despite his special needs.

The golden hour arrived. Mark and Luke stood at the open front door. An extended-cab pickup pulled up to the curb outside, closely followed by a flashy red sports car. A young woman in black leather pants and heels stepped out of the sports car and walked down our driveway to a middle-aged couple emerging from the pickup. They opened the passenger side of the extended cab as the golden lab-mix from the picture tentatively leaped to the ground. The man firmly held JoJo by a leash. Mark and Luke walked onto the porch exchanging greetings and introductions.

Mark busied Luke with holding the doors to allow everyone inside. The man and his wife walked JoJo into our living room, followed by the young woman in leather pants. Luke sat near JoJo petting him and letting him smell his hand; he was squinting away tears of joy. I heard Matthew stirring, then tapping on his baby gate. I went to check on him and bring him out to meet JoJo.

"What's going on, Matthew? What's all the noise you hear? Let's go see!" I said.

Matthew looked curiously down the hall toward the voices spilling from our living room. I walked him down the hallway toward the living room and pulled him into my lap, a safe distance from where Luke sat contentedly petting JoJo. I introduced Matthew to everyone. Matthew sat in my lap, glancing curiously at JoJo from his peripheral vision and then quickly looking away.

"What do you think, Matthew?" I asked him. "It's a dog in our house; his name is JoJo." Matthew continued his peripheral glancing and looking away. Slowly and gingerly, I scooted closer to JoJo so Matthew could touch his fluffy tail. Slowly, I took Matthew's hand and extended it hand-over-hand to JoJo's tail. Matthew touched it, lightly fingered JoJo's tail fluff, and pulled his hand away. I was pleased he had tried.

The pet adoption lady wanted to ensure we had an appropriately fenced backyard, so everyone headed outside with JoJo. The couple was pleased for JoJo and his new home; the pet adoption lady was happy as well. She wanted to be certain we could handle walking Jojo on a leash, so she, Mark, Luke, and the couple headed for the park with Jojo.

I seized the opportunity to claim the few moments of calm for both my sake and Matthew's. I was glad we were getting a dog for Luke. I was unsure how the new dog would respond to Matthew and vice versa. My old misgivings about the extra workload rose to the surface again, but I swatted them away. Mark had promised Luke a dog, and he must make good on his promise. I was glad Mark had come through, and I was thrilled for Luke. I would manage this added responsibility along with all the rest, and in time, I would warm up to the idea of a dog.

Mark, Luke, and the fostering couple returned from the park, walking JoJo through the side gate into the backyard. The pet adoption lady produced the clipboard of papers for Mark to sign and left. Mark ran JoJo a fresh bowl of water from the hose as everyone sat on the grass. The man eased off JoJo's leash, allowing Luke and JoJo to scamper about the yard together. JoJo was smiling, and Luke grinned from ear to ear.

The couple decided to slip away while JoJo was distracted. As they turned to leave, the woman cast a wistful glance toward JoJo and Luke as they played. The man urged her forward. "He's in good hands. He'll be just fine," he said to her. She nodded, squinting away tears. They passed quickly through our front door and down the drive.

Matthew and I watched and waited from the front porch. The woman opened the passenger side of the extended cab, retrieved a gaudy gold comforter covered with red and pink roses, and handed it to Mark. It was JoJo's dog bed at their house, she said. She also handed Mark a bag of dog food along with a few cans of wet dog food. She mentioned how she hated to give JoJo up, but her medical issues made it a necessity. She was squinting away tears again; her husband urged her into the truck. She complied and they quickly drove away. Mark and I waved as they drove away.

Mark went to check on Luke and JoJo. Matthew and I joined them in the backyard to become further acquainted with our new dog. Luke and JoJo scampered and played in the backyard until supper time. Mark fixed JoJo's food as the fostering couple had instructed. He was too distracted and discombobulated to settle down and eat. He did lap water from his bowl and wander about his new house. Luke took the gold comforter and fluffed it out on his bedroom floor for JoJo. Luke and JoJo lay together on the gold comforter, bonding throughout the evening as I worked Matthew and the rest of the family through our regular routine.

Matthew continued his pattern of sideways glances at JoJo and quickly looking away. He did so throughout the evening. He was working hard to process the idea of a dog in our house. I continued working Matthew through his regular routine, and thankfully, he drifted off to sleep without incident. Luke urged JoJo to lie in his room on the gold comforter. JoJo complied, and Luke drifted off to sleep dreaming happy dreams of a boy with his dog.

I was awakened throughout the night to let JoJo outside. I did my best to resettle him on the gold comforter, but I was certain he was most likely hungry since he hadn't eaten the night before. JoJo finally settled in the corner of the dining room. He was still sleeping soundly in that place when I got up early the next morning. By the end of day two, he began to eat again, and we were well on our way to adjusting to life as dog owners.

JoJo seemed confused, and sad, yet resigned to his new family—at least for the first week. He soon discovered that not only were we nice people, but he had an entire yard to himself with a family thrown in. He also discovered my vegetable garden and enjoyed lolling beneath the canopy of bean vines, as well as the pleasure of a sunlit nap in my flower bed full of well-tended, blooming dianthus. He seemed to assume I planted them just so he could lie among the soft, fragrant blooms and seemed perplexed that they went away, as section by section, they died from being smashed. JoJo quickly became part of the family mix, and his name JoJo, gradually morphed into Joey. Like most families who adopt a pet, the pet chores that Luke insisted he would perform with regularity and exuberance soon fell upon Mark or me.

Luke and Joey quickly became friends. Joey was never inappropriate with Matthew but preferred to keep his distance. Since Joey was a big dog, he did not tolerate heat well and needed to be in air conditioning during the long summer afternoons. He found his safe place away from Matthew at the end of the hallway. I spent many long summer afternoons keeping Matthew safe and occupied in the living room as Joey napped at the end of the hallway.

As usual, after his romp at the lake for church family camp, Luke spent the remainder of his summer at the neighborhood pool, riding bikes, and playing with friends at the nearby park. He came and went throughout the day, telling me he was going back to the park, pool, or creek. He'd get a drink and a few popsicles to share with friends and was off again.

Matthew attended summer school for half days in June. For the remainder of the summer, he and I were simply at home together. Since we'd installed full-length doors to block off the kitchen for safety reasons, he and I were confined to the living room area or Matthew's bedroom unless he was secured in his wheelchair. I continued to wheel him into the kitchen in his wheelchair if I was cooking, cleaning, or working there. He seemed to enjoy that I talked to him as I worked and that he was part of whatever I was doing. When he and I were not hanging out in the kitchen, we were simply together in the living room. To keep myself awake, I often turned on a rom-com movie, caught up on a favorite news show, or tried to work out with an exercise program. During my exercise programs, he clamored about me and flopped on top of me during floor work, or rolled about underfoot during aerobics. Mostly, he would wander around stimming with his favorite toys, dragging his blue blanket while making his characteristic swooshing noise. However, he still stopped at the tall windows to watch the hummingbirds and butterflies from his peripheral vision. I often joined him at the window, where he'd back up to me and plop into my lap as we watched the shimmering hummingbirds dive-bomb one another as they fought for territorial control of the feeder. A tiny green female Luke and I dubbed "Queenie Meanie" often held her watch post on a nearby branch, deftly swooping after would-be invaders.

On other summer afternoons, Matthew would nap on the living room floor or couch with his blue blanket. As he napped, I often slipped into the kitchen to hear a sermon from one of my "pastor friends" or steal a few moments of quietness alone at the kitchen counter with my Bible, leaving the door open as Matthew slept. I often read of heaven and the Apostle Paul's hardships, marveling as he referred to them as "light and momentary."

However, the more I read of heaven, the more I understood. This life is not all there is; eternity is real—more real, in fact, than this life. There is more to come and our earthly life is a mere episode in the grand drama of God's eternal story. This perspective offered a shift that lifted my focus from the weightiness of my circumstances to the glory and crown awaiting us. If the Apostle Paul viewed his heaviest circumstances as "light and momentary" through this lens, then so could I.

This eternal perspective hit home one hot afternoon. It was one of those days when seizures were escalating and Matthew struggled to eat and drink as the meds and seizures left him dazed and exhausted. As I patiently worked to feed him, I spoke to him softly of another world, more real than this one, where there are no seizures and special needs. "It won't always be this way, Buddy. It won't always be this way," I said. In a quiet corner of my mind, the faintly whispered reminder arose: "Matthew won't always be here with us." Hymn lyrics rose to my lips as I sang him one of his favorite songs of heaven:

"Shall we gather at the river, where bright angel feet have trod; with its crystal tide forever, flowing by the throne of God? Yes, we'll gather at the river, the beautiful river, gather with the saints at the river, that flows by the throne of God!"

As I sang, I knew he would beat me to that beautiful river; he would walk where angel feet have trod and behold the face of my Jesus before I did. However, as the hymn declared, he and I would indeed gather at that river together someday. Through streaming tears, in a trembling voice, and with brazen faith, I sang on. I declared the bright truth of Scripture in song despite the droning sadness and gathering gloom of another afternoon on the long haul on this stunningly difficult road.

"On the bosom of the river, where the Savior-King we own, we shall meet and sorrow never, 'neath the glory of the throne."

My heart both exalted and ached for the coming days of embracing my Savior-King and no sorrow. I belted out the refrain again through tears and in faith; Matthew rested his head against the back of his blue wheelchair, listening and smiling. I sang on:

"Soon we'll reach the shining river, soon our pilgrimage will cease; soon our happy hearts will quiver with the melody of peace. Yes, we'll gather at the river, the beautiful the beautiful river, gather with the saints at the river that flows by the throne of God."

My heart soared and broke at the same time. I felt like I was telling him what would soon happen, and in a way, I was. I sang the last verse for him again, changing the wording, making it personal, and pointing him towards what lay ahead—hoping in faith that on some level he understood me.

*"Soon **you'll** reach the shining river, soon **your** pilgrimage will cease, soon **your** happy will quiver with the melody of peace. Yes, **you'll** gather at the river, the beautiful, the beautiful river, gather with the saints at the river that flows by the throne of God."*

I talked to him softly of heaven. I asked him to be sure and throw his arms around my Jesus for me, tell Him how I loved Him and how I couldn't wait to run into His arms. I laughed through my tears as I teased Matthew that it wasn't fair that he got to see Jesus first. He just rested his head and listened as I spoke. I rejoiced with eyes of faith peering over the horizon to both the robust health and happiness awaiting not just Matthew, but us all. My tears were for the painful realities of that hot afternoon in our kitchen and in anticipation of the painful separation ahead.

This eternity-focused mindset fueled my perseverance. Through this lens, I could press on despite desperate circumstances. I could persist in stalwart faith– often reaching through my ongoing discouragement to grasp tightly to the truth of Scripture even though circumstances touted the opposite message. Knowing there was a greater purpose in our suffering infused me with the courage to press forward and hold on in faith. I will never know the purpose for Matthew's illnesses and special needs on this side of Heaven. Yet through the eyes of faith, I could stand on tip-toe, gazing over the horizon toward eternity knowing that life's "light and momentary trials" truly are storing up for Matthew, and me, a crown of righteousness that God will award us on that day.

Despite the undergirding strength and perspective these mindsets provided, the realities on the ground, seemingly, ran cross-grain to the truth of Scripture. Real questions loitered in my head, as they politely raised issues like this:

- Scripture states repeatedly that God is good, kind, compassionate, and loving, yet Matthew continued suffering with severe special needs, seizures, and countless other medical issues. How could a good, compassionate, and loving God allow my helpless boy to suffer?

- Scripture relays account after account of Jesus healing the sick, raising the dead, and bringing all sorts of comfort and deliverance from illness and long-term disability. God has the power to heal completely, yet Matthew continued to suffer, despite my fervent, ongoing prayers.

- Scripture is clear that God hears each prayer, listens to our heart's cries, and answers them in His ultimate wisdom. However, despite my constant prayers for Matthew's healing and deliverance in this life, His answer was "No." His "No" was promptly followed by: "My grace is sufficient for you; my power is made perfect in weakness. . ." Frankly, it felt more like a cruel non-answer.

Living in that limbo land of questions with no satisfactory answers is an odd dwelling place. It often felt akin to betrayal or like I'd been duped. The comfort and perspective people offered sounded like hokey sentimentality. The evil one stood ready to hijack my faith and drive me to the nowhere-land of bitterness and disillusionment with God and the whole notion of faith. The evil one desired to kill my faith in God and take me out in the process. Jeeringly, he pointed out the incongruities of my harsh and painful circumstances and what looked and felt like God's inattention and cruelty. This was his practice since the boys were babies, and he clearly had no intention of relenting. If he could take me out, he could take out my entire family. As in former days, he loitered still, yet it often seemed I could feel his hot foul breath upon me as he patiently waited for an opportune moment to attack.

However, Jesus's recurring question to me through His Word was: "Do you trust me?" His ongoing assertion was: "This life is not all there is. I'm doing something bigger. I will never leave you. I am here. There is no need to be afraid." His words were mostly about a trusting relationship with Him; nothing was said about changing circumstances in my favor.

I began to settle upon the fact that answers were not going to come, yet that reality was not a deal-breaker between us. My heart echoed Peter's declaration in Scripture: ". ...where else can we go, as You have the words of life?" The main issue in my heart and soul was trusting the One who was in control of the process rather than knowing what was next. As long as I knew my Jesus was in full control and had my boys and me in His arms, that was enough for me.

Along the way, it was becoming difficult—even impossible—for us to attend church as a family. Though our church worked hard to serve our family's unique circumstances, Matthew's needs were becoming increasingly difficult to manage. For a while, we worked with volunteers who served Matthew and our family valiantly; however, it wasn't long before we were forced to keep Matthew at home. Once again, unselfish church friends watched Matthew at our house so we could attend church together as a family once or twice per month.

As summer slipped away and the "back to school" sales started, as usual, an unsettled restlessness settled over me. The reprieve of summer had ended, and I had to return to school. I always dreaded the beginning of school and the return to the classroom and hoped Mark would make the magical pronouncement that my working outside the home was no longer necessary. Dutifully, I attended the series of meetings, professional development, and convocation, and the new school year started for me in a brand new building.

Like other moms of school-age kids, I packed lunches the night before. Luke's lunch was a typical sack lunch, but Matthew's consisted of two bottles of clear Kool-Aid thickened with gel thickener and a portion of whatever we had for supper pureed to the consistency of thick applesauce. I packed it into brightly colored Tupperware sectioned lunch containers, placed it with a cold pack into the blue and red Spiderman lunchbox, a hand-me-down from Luke, and stowed it in the fridge.

In the early morning hours, I got myself ready for school, listening to Scripture on my Bible app as I did so. I finished packing the boys' lunches and loaded the backpacks. I made Matthew a bowl of his maple and brown sugar oatmeal, his favorite, set it aside to cool and laid out his morning meds. It always seemed cruel to wake him for school, but it was among many of the necessary displeasures of our day. I often diapered him as he was waking up, and carried him half-sleeping to his feeding chair. I worked hard to coax him to eat, slipping the pills and meds into each spoonful of oatmeal. Sometimes he swallowed it, and other times he pocketed the food and pills in his mouth, requiring me to massage his throat, coaxing him to swallow. With the meds and breakfast down the hatch, I carried him back to his bedroom, changed, and dressed him for school. His blue crash helmet and the bus harness were the final steps before bus time. In winter months, the coat went on first, then the harness. He often fell asleep on his bedroom floor bundled into his coat and harness while we waited for the bus.

I made sure Luke was up and getting around for school and waited for Matthew's bus. Sometimes Matthew fell back asleep during the wait, other times he was amped up and required my hands-on assistance to stay safe in his room as we waited. Other times, he lay on the floor and soaked his diaper and school clothes as I helped Luke get around for school, requiring a quick call to the bus driver to explain and a quick change and re-do of the coat and harness process. Once Matthew was on his bus and headed to school, I could focus on finishing the process of getting Luke and myself around for school. Like most parents, some mornings went smoothly, while others required extra prodding and pushing as Luke's sleepiness, distraction, and pokiness slowed our morning routine. Once Luke was headed to the corner toward school with his friends, I had a few minutes to finish getting ready for my day and head out for work at my building. As I scrambled to get to work on time, an exhausted prayer often rose from my frenzied mind: "Lord, this is insane. I'm already exhausted. When does this madness end? Give me strength for today, because the madness remains for today."

As in other buildings, I worked as a paraprofessional in a high-needs classroom. What I did in the classroom mirrored what I did at home with Matthew. The stress of being in a new building with new teachers and staff pressed hard upon me, pushing me near a breaking point. I rejoiced in the knowledge that I was on half-days and pushed through until lunchtime when I could leave.

With the boys and me scattered among three different school buildings and two different school districts, school picture day often eluded me for one of us. After a typical night of settling and resettling Matthew and letting the dog in or out, I decided to start my day well before daybreak. I finished packing lunches and backpacks, readied the boys' clothes, and got them off to school as usual. I checked the clock, realizing the morning had scooted away from me. I had only a few minutes to get ready and leave for school. I dabbed on some makeup, brushed, sprayed, and fluffed my unwashed hair. I dressed in a pair of work slacks and an orange tee shirt from the top of the folded clean laundry basket, crammed my feet in my shoes. Grabbing my purse and keys, I was off to another school day.

I arrived at school as usual to find a stream of perfectly coiffed teachers and paras streaming toward the photographer's station in the activity center. I dove into a nearby restroom, fumbling in my purse for a powder compact and lipstick—anything that may help. The school secretary's message broke in, "All teachers and paras, please head to the activity center for pictures. Smile pretty for your pictures!" The bathroom door opened, and a co-worker joined me in the mirror. She eyed me in my orange tee shirt, and limp hair as I furiously powdered my nose and swiped on lipstick.

"Did you know it was picture day?" she asked. I shook my head. "Nice!" she said. She fluffed her hair and left. I slinked toward the activity center, waited my turn, and sat for my school picture in my orange tee shirt and all my bedraggled glory. Embarrassed, I tried to forget the incident.

One morning, as I was gathering craft supplies in the teacher's workroom, a co-worker handed me a picture envelope, and she distributed photos of the staff from picture day. I was afraid to look, so I tucked the envelope under my arm, slipped it into my purse, and went on with my day.

I completed my school day and prepared to leave, slinging my purse into the passenger seat. Peering through the cellophane window of the picture envelope was the sun-kissed farmgirl—orange dress traded for an orange tee shirt. It startled me. I sucked in my breath. I hadn't thought of her in years. I wondered if she still lived.

I headed home. At the stoplight near our house, I sat waiting, listening to the loud clicking of my turn signal. The farmgirl continued smiling up at me from the windowed envelope tucked into the top of my purse. Tears stung my eyes. The girlhood dream born in the sunlit garden seemed so far away—so lost, forgotten—so gone. I turned into our driveway. It was a sunny afternoon, so I set my purse on the grass and momentarily checked my flower bed. The orange and yellow marigolds leaned toward me heavy with ruffled blooms. Tucked among the vibrant blossoms were spent blooms dried into seed pods. I plucked them off, scratching a crude furrow into the soil with a nearby rock. I crushed the dried seed pods sprinkling the black and white, stick-like seeds into my crude furrow, and patted the earth over them, as I often did. Whether they flourished and bloomed this season or next, there they rested where the magic between seed and soil transpires.

Dusting my hands on my pants, I turned to leave. I reached for my purse from where I'd left it, and there she was again, smiling back at me—the farmgirl. She lived on among the seeds and soil. In that place where He does His best work, where trusting surrender meets obedient faith, the farmgirl waited in enduring hope. The precious dream had long since been given over to her Heavenly

Father for safekeeping, and there it lived on beneath His watchful and tender eye. However, it was no longer hers—it was *theirs* now—a priceless treasure shared between Father and daughter.

As I set about the tasks of getting lunch for Mark and me, packing his lunch, and sending him off to work, a quiet peace settled over me. The farmgirl in her orange dress seemed to linger near as I went about my household chores. We were one now, joined in the brokenness of crushed dreams, joined in the simple beauty of seed and soil, joined in the slow crushing within His hands as He births something new.

Mark left for work by 2 PM and I had forty precious minutes alone before Matthew's bus time. I often shifted into overdrive finishing up dishes, starting laundry, or wiping down bathrooms as I listened to one of my "pastor friends" on the kitchen radio. As usual, our evening routine was driven by Matthew's med schedule and need for routine. Whatever I made for Luke and me for supper, I plopped into the food processor and pureed for Matthew. Luke and I often joked about the multi-colored goop Matthew ate, but he seemed to like his favorite flavors even in their pasty form. He was always up for a pasta casserole, meat, potatoes and gravy, sweet potatoes, ham and bean soup, lentil and sausage soup, sauerkraut, and brats. He also liked sweets and homemade gingersnaps soaked in milk, which were among his favorites.

By this time, my bathing Matthew in the bathtub had become an exhausting and unsafe ordeal for both of us, so I moved him to the shower. We used the same foam visor he'd always used since he was a toddler to keep the water and soap out of his eyes, and he spun in circles in the shower spray as I scrubbed him up and down and washed his nut-brown hair. I wrapped him in a giant towel and lugged him to his room for a diaper, lotion, and jammies. The shower often worked well, until his seizure escalated with illness.

One evening when he was ill, I questioned whether the shower was a good idea given his tendency to fall either straight backward or straight forward when he seized. I knew it would require hands-on vigilance, but decided to take a chance for the sake of sticking to a routine. I readied him for the shower, walked him in, and turned on the water, keeping the sliding shower door open to keep a hand on him as he spun about in the shower spray. I quickly shampooed his hair and soaped his body. As I rinsed the shampoo from his hair, he threw up his arms and stiffened in his usual manner at the onset of a seizure. I caught his wet, soapy body with my forearm, flung open the shower door with my knee, and flipped off the shower with my other hand. He slumped against me as I sat fully clothed on the shower floor. I noted the duration and type of seizure as usual, and he relaxed against me as the seizure passed. I rested my head against the shower wall, holding his wet soapy body in my lap, planning my course of action. I called for Luke. He came, staring in shock at Matthew collapsed, naked, and soapy, and me holding him as I sat soaked and fully clothed in the shower.

"Brother had a seizure in the shower. I caught him before he hit his head. I need that tall cup on the counter filled with warm water," I said. Luke filled it and brought it to me with a questioning look. I poured the water over Matthew, rinsing away the soap. I asked Luke to bring me a towel, and he did so. I wrapped Matthew in it and carried him to his room. Luke followed, curious and concerned.

Water dripped from my hair, and my wet T-shirt stuck to my back as Luke helped me towel off Matthew. I diapered Matthew and Luke helped me dress him and lay him on his bed to recover. Luke lay beside him, patting his arm and shoulder as he lay exhausted and limp.

"Buddy, stay with Brother while I change these wet clothes," I said. I grabbed dry clothes and stepped into the bathroom, peeling off the soggy tee and sweats and putting on the dry clothes. I stared into the mirror as I combed out my half-wet hair. "That could've been so much worse," I mused. "I have to figure out a better way to shower him and still keep him safe." His seizures were not going away; they were our daily reality. He also needed to be bathed or showered. I thanked God for keeping him safe and for helping me act quickly, but I also knew it was going to be part of our lives. He would continue to get sick and he would continue to have seizures. It was just another instance in our lives that required my hands-on vigilance to ensure his safety.

Our weeks and months flowed along at this taxing pace, highlighted by our Monday evening reprieve from my church friend Cynthia. She came faithfully each Monday evening to provide respite from the ongoing demands of Matthew's care. Cynthia was also a physical therapist and well-versed in caring for special needs children. She could skillfully take over for me and handle the entire evening routine. Matthew was comfortable enough with her that he would sometimes go to sleep for the night while she was with him, and not wait for me to come home. Sometimes Cynthia brought her son and daughter along, and they quickly became good friends with Luke. I was simply grateful for the opportunity to leave the house alone for a trip to Walmart or the grocery store. Sometimes I just went to the basement and spent time alone.

Aside from Cynthia's Monday evening respite visits, our extremely stressful and demanding pace continued unabated, except when Matthew was ill and the seizures kicked into overdrive once again. In those instances, he and I were back in the hospital, handling whatever illness tipped the carefully balanced scales and readjusting seizure medications as needed.

FOOD FOR THOUGHT:

1. When life's journey turns into an expectedly long haul, what has kept you moving forward? What Scriptures undergird you and give you strength and hope when giving up or slipping into despair seems like easier options?

2. What realities of your life seem to cut across the grain of Scripture? What conversations do you and God have about them? What is He saying to you? How do you feel about His answers—or lack thereof?

CHAPTER 9

MY STRENGTH IN MAJOR DOWNTURNS

"For I am sure that neither death nor life, nor angels nor rulers, nor things present nor things to come, nor powers, nor height nor depth, nor anything else in all creation, will be able to separate us from the love of God in Christ Jesus our Lord."

Romans 8:38–39, ESV

"We are afflicted in every way, but not crushed; perplexed, but not driven to despair; persecuted, but not forsaken; struck down, but not destroyed; . . ."

2 Corinthians 4:8–9, ESV

I n the spring of 2011, Matthew got sick once again with another round of upper respiratory illness. His fever continued, but a quick visit to his primary doctor ruled out strep, so she sent us home with a regular round of antibiotics. They helped somewhat, but something else was going on. His fever abated and his antibiotics ran their course, so with hesitation, I sent him back to school.

I followed my morning routine, got Luke off to school, and was driving to school when I got a voicemail from Matthew's bus driver saying he was having seizures on the bus and they were taking him back to his school building to be with the school nurse. I should come to get him as soon as possible. I sat in the school parking lot, listened to the message again, and then went into the building to speak with my principal. I found her hustling into an early morning meeting and briefly told her my situation. She excused me, and I left the building and headed for Matthew's school.

When I got there, the receptionist hurried me back to the nurses' office where Matthew was lying on a bed, clearly worn out from seizing. His backpack, coat, and bus harness lay piled against the wall near his feet. Matthew had started having seizures on their way back to the school, and the driver stopped at the school building to drop him off with the nurse and continued on her route. No one knew how many seizures he'd had or their duration. He'd had one since being dropped off at the school. The receptionist and other administrators hovered nearby, obviously concerned. I thanked the nurses and administrators, put Matthew into his coat, slung his backpack on my shoulder, and took him home.

Matthew's congestion escalated and his fever returned. I called the nurse line at our primary care physician's office and I did my best to control the fever and congestion with over-the-counter medication. He refused to settle down and sleep and seemed more comfortable sitting up in his wheelchair, so I strapped him in and kept him near me as I worked around the house for the remainder of the day.

I followed my evening routine, showering him with the same hands-on vigilance, slathering him with lotion, and dressing him in fresh jammies, hoping for a sound night's sleep and a better day tomorrow. He refused to settle; I tried calming deep pressure and singing. Nothing worked. I was in for a long night. The garage door buzzed; Mark was home. I heard him on the basement stairs. He stood quietly in the hallway outside Matthew's room.

"How's he doing?" he whispered. "Any better?"

I came into the hallway to speak with him. "He's had a rough day," I said. "Something isn't right. It's more than a bad cold or sinus crud. I don't know what to do." Mark nodded and disappeared into the bedroom. He handed me the hospital bag. "Just in case you need it," he said. "Wake me up if you go or if you need help." He closed the door and went to bed.

I returned to Matthew. His congestion was escalating once again. He could not lie down comfortably. An elevated pile of pillows helped temporarily but did not solve the problem. He wanted to be up and moving. There was something oddly familiar in his behavior. I watched intently as he spun about his room. Then he suddenly stopped. He stood still, his chest heaving up and down. He couldn't breathe–pneumonia!

I woke Mark enough to tell him what was happening, grabbed my hospital bag, and jammed my feet into my shoes as I located my purse and keys. I scooped up Matthew, buckled him into the car seat, and dialed the nurse line for the emergency room as I pulled out. I snaked through the empty streets and onto the interstate. The receptionist answered. I relayed the events of the evening; I was bringing Matthew in for possible pneumonia. We would be there within ten minutes, I told her, and hung up.

I swung into a parking spot under a street light, unbuckled Matthew, and lugged him up the hill towards the lighted Emergency Room sign. The security guard in a white shirt asked for my

ID and wheeled up a transport wagon. I lay Matthew in the wagon and dug in my purse for my wallet, producing an ID. He printed the adhesive badge and I slapped it onto the front of my sweater, wheeling Matthew into the nearly empty waiting room. I mentioned my phone call to the receptionist and she moved us directly into a side room. She clipped an oxygen probe onto his finger and began the usual protocol of questions about medications, height, and weight. She wanted to get a current and accurate weight, so I lifted him out of the wagon and onto the scale. He stared at me blankly, his chest heaving up and down, the nurse eyed his oxygen saturation: it was in the high 80s. As he stood wobbling on the scale, his arms flew outward, as his body stiffened in a seizure. I knew he would fall backward, and braced myself to catch him. The nurse stared at me as I scooped him into my lap.

"That was a seizure. Is that what his seizures normally look like?" she asked. I nodded and mentioned that they escalated whenever he was sick. She nodded, writing in his chart as she opened the door leading into the emergency room.

"I'll be right back," she said. "Let me see what room is available." She disappeared around the corner, and I could hear her talking to someone at the nurses' station. She reappeared in the doorway. "Let's get you guys in here," she said, pointing to the exam room directly across from the nurses' station. I wheeled Matthew in the wagon; the nurse carried my purse, hospital bag, and Matthew's backpack. We had been here before.

I lifted Matthew onto the gurney as the nurse placed the oxygen cannula under his nose. Almost immediately a doctor came to speak with me. She examined Matthew and confirmed the seizure the nurse witnessed. She ordered lab work and a chest X-ray. The nurse pulled a hospital gown from a drawer in the unit. I took it from her and busied myself changing him into it and stowing his clothes into his backpack in the wagon. I scooted a chair next to Matthew's gurney and waited. His gaze rested on me; it was pathetic, with an exhausted "help me" air about it. I rose and stood near him. I laid my cheek against his forehead. It was still warm with a fever; his oxygen still hovered in the high 80's to low 90's. Tears stung my eyes and I blinked them away.

"Lord, what's going on? Pneumonia–again? Help him breathe; help me know what to do, what to say, what to ask the doctors," I prayed.

There was a tap on the sliding glass door, two lab techs in blue scrubs stood there, one wheeled a caddy full of supplies. "Lab work for Matthew?" the tech asked. I nodded and waved them in. The tech tapped the inside of Matthew's elbow, looking for a good vein while the other searched for a vein in his wrist and hands. They opted for the right arm and prepped for the stick. I knew my role in the process. I caught Matthew's eye as I laid my body across his, securing his left arm beneath me, and began to sing.

I eyed the tech and gave him the okay. The other tech rubbed the spot with an alcohol swab and steadied Matthew's arm. The other tech tapped the vein again and gave the countdown–3, 2, 1, and stick. The needle was in but no blood flowed into the tubing. He moved the needle slightly, and Matthew grimaced and yelled, but the blood began to flow into the tubing and the vials. The tech labeled each vial and placed them in her caddy. She produced a blue arm board. The two of them taped Matthew's arm into an extended position on the board and secured his IV in place. They gathered their caddy and were gone.

Matthew was still half awake, gazing at me with the same "help me" look. I stood near him, smoothing his hair, and pressed my cheek against his forehead as I held his hand. I breathed in and out, letting the inarticulate groaning of my soul rise to heaven. The beeping monitors sounded far away. I felt myself sinking into sleep but was powerless against the pull, so I let it pull me away.

"X-ray for Matthew?" I jolted awake. It was a radiology tech. "We'll have to take him down to the machine as the portable machine is unavailable," she explained. "He can walk down there, right?" she asked.

"I can carry him," I said. "How far is it?" The tech pointed down the hall. Our nurse appeared, removed Matthew's oxygen cannula, and helped me lift him, wheeling his IV pole behind me.

Matthew would have to stand against a metal plate for the X-ray, facing forward and then facing backward. The nurse helped me place Matthew against the metal plate and hold his arms out of the way. As he stood, his knees wobbled beneath him; the tech handed out the heavy black aprons and gave the countdown. It was done. The nurse helped me reverse Matthew's position; his knees nearly buckled in weakness. The tech gave the countdown once again, and it was done. The nurse eyed me sadly as I lifted Matthew once again. He slumped heavily against me as I lugged him back to our unit. Our nurse followed, wheeling his IV pole and placing the oxygen cannula back under his nose.

"Do you need anything?" she asked me. My mind was blank, so I shook my head and took up my post beside Matthew's gurney. Matthew continued to lie half awake, with his cloudy gaze settled upon me. He was resting more easily with the oxygen cannula back in place.

The doctor tapped on the sliding glass door. "Hi, we spoke earlier," she said. I nodded. "X-rays confirm pneumonia in both lobes," she said. "This seems different from his past round of pneumonia; this one seems bacterial rather than viral. We're working on getting him a room upstairs. We'll need to keep him here for several days until he's out of the woods and doing better. He's in the right place, and we'll get him on the right track soon. Poor guy," she said and turned to leave. Our nurse hovered nearby; she and the doctor talked quietly and the doctor left. Matthew was finally sleeping. A band of tightness clenched the back of my neck, and slipped up the left side of my head, digging in its claws.

Our nurse came and went to check Matthew's oxygen levels and adjust them as needed. "Are you sure I can't bring you something? A water? Some crackers?" I nodded. "Perhaps I can find an ibuprofen pill in my purse," I mused. I rummaged in my purse and found a travel-sized pill bottle and dumped my usual dosage into my hand, waiting for the nurse to bring the water bottle. Our nurse returned, handing me a kid-sized water bottle and a packet of saltine crackers. I took it gratefully, washed down my pills, and ate the cracker.

Our nurse poked her head in, saying the transport team was on their way down. We'd be headed upstairs to a room soon. I gathered my purse, hospital bag, and Matthew's backpack and returned the wagon to the nurses' station. I stood beside Matthew's gurney and waited. The transport team arrived. It was the same fit crew in the navy jumpsuits. They deftly transferred Matthew from his gurney to the hospital bed. Someone grabbed his IV pole and I followed him to the waiting transport elevator. We all crowded in, Matthew remained asleep. A team member placed his chart on the foot of his bed. I closed my eyes and leaned against the elevator wall. The elevator thudded to a stop, the door slid open, and I stepped out into the familiar elevator lobby and stood aside as the transport team wheeled Matthew off the elevator. They stopped at the nurse's station, handing off the chart from the end of his bed, receiving his room assignment, and wheeling him toward his room.

It was a familiar room. I set down my purse, hospital bag, and Matthew's backpack on the couch near the window and stared out at the darkness. I had no idea what time it was. I'd left the house with Matthew before midnight; the clock on the DVD player said 4-something AM. Nurses came and went asking me questions and settling Matthew as usual. I sank into the blue recliner and waited. Nurses began hovering longer than usual, and traded the oxygen cannula for a mask, waiting and watching with quiet concern. I watched and listened. "Is everything okay besides the pneumonia?" I asked.

"We're concerned and watching him closely," the nurse said. "We're calling a doctor to look him over and calling about a possible transfer to PICU."

Doctor returning? Pneumonia? PICU? This sounded too familiar! A hard knot settled in my gut.

A woman in a white lab coat came in. "You must be Matthew's mom," she said. "Yes, we're concerned for Matthew. He's got a nasty strain of bacterial pneumonia, and he's struggling. He needs more help than the regular nursing floor can provide. I'm getting the transport team back and we'll move him downstairs to PICU." She spoke quietly to the nurses and was gone.

My head throbbed, and swam in confusion. Tears stung my eyes. I squinted them away. Numbly, I shouldered my hospital bag, purse, and Matthew's backpack once again, stood by his bedside, and waited. I fingered his soft brown hair and pushed the heel of my hand hard against my mouth to push down the sobs threatening to burst out. I squeezed my abdominal muscles firmly to keep myself from bursting into tears.

The transport team arrived, greeting me: "Us again; you two again." I nodded and tried hard to smile. With their same swiftness and skill, Matthew and I were on the move once again, cramming into the transport elevator. A team member was punching a series of buttons and we were plunging downward to the PICU. The elevator bumped to a stop and the door opened, early morning light illuminated the same beige hallway, the same series of double doors opened and the transport team wheeled Matthew into the same glassed-in unit he'd been in before. I backed out of the way, as the transport team transferred Matthew into the care of the PICU team. I spotted my old friend, the green recliner, pushed into the corner against the wall. A nurse approached, suggesting I may be more comfortable in the waiting room until Matthew was settled. I nodded, retraced my steps through the double doors, and settled once more in the same darkened corner of the waiting room. I sank into a chair and leaned back against the wall. It was after 5 AM, and I could text Mark within forty minutes and call him after that. My headache lessened. I leaned back against the wall, resting my head and letting the bags slip to the floor by my feet. I tried to pray but couldn't. I couldn't think coherently, so I just leaned back against the wall and waited.

"Matthew's mom?" It was the receptionist. I jumped up and waved, shouldering my bags once again. The receptionist buzzed me through the double doors once again and I was back in Matthew's unit. The nurse mentioned the various antibiotics Matthew was on and how they would help. I lifted the sheet to see the same pressure cuffs squeezing his legs. He was sleeping soundly, and an oxygen mask was on his mouth and nose. His right arm lay extended, taped securely to the blue arm board placed by the lab techs in the emergency room. Bags of fluids and syringes of medicine hung from the IV pole nearby and flowed into the port fastened with clear adhesive in his right arm. I asked the nurse if I could drag the green recliner from the corner for a place to sit. She nodded and came to help me scoot it into a place near Matthew, yet out of the way of the nurses and doctors.

I sank into the recliner. We were back. I hadn't seen it coming. My eyes burned as I stared numbly at the reality before me. The nurse reminded me of the Ronald McDonald Parent Facility down the beige hallway. I nodded and walked the familiar route I'd walked before. I reserved a room and was immediately back in my PICU routine. I stowed my bags in my room and went back to Matthew's unit to text Mark an update. He was stunned and shaken. He'd get Luke to school and handle things at home.

The days that followed were a blur. I ate and did my laundry in the Ronald McDonald Parent's Room. I sat in the green recliner, wrote email updates for friends and family, and waited to talk with Matthew's doctor each morning. One day the doctor said he could return to the regular nursing floor, but would likely be there for at least a week. I was glad he was improving, but knew he had a long recovery ahead.

A team of nurses from the regular nursing floor came down to retrieve Matthew and bring him up to a room on their floor. It was one of our old rooms with a familiar staff. Our nurse indicated that the doctor had said that Matthew would be here recovering for at least a week to ten days. I began to make assessments of our situation and how things may be different once we got home. I contacted my process coordinator at our Regional Center and the hospital social worker to check if available funding sources might enable me to stay home with Matthew rather than return to the workplace. My process coordinator stopped by the hospital; there was no funding for me to stay home, but there were funding sources for adaptive equipment for the home. I immediately applied. The hospital social worker and I visited. She helped me apply for funding to stay home. I would be denied, she said, but it was the first of a series of hoops we would be expected to jump through. It was denied; at least I had tried.

I could see the lay of the land going forward from this hospitalization would be different. We could no longer proceed as usual; I needed to quit my job at school and be more rested and available to care for Matthew as his level of care was only increasing. I had to do what I could on my end; it led to a dead end. Day after day, I sat in Matthew's hospital room trying to figure it all out as I listened to Scripture on my Bible app, journaled, and tried hard to pray. I settled once again into my hospital routine. I made the couch into a bed each evening. I gazed up at the night sky through the nearby window and talked to my Jesus as I drifted off to sleep in the glow of light from the hallway. There were no eloquent prayers, mostly it was wordless groaning rising from my battle-weary soul as tears slipped silently into the pillowcase on the hospital pillow.

Nurses on the unit expressed their kindness and concern, noting that I had not been home or had decent nights' sleep since Matthew and I came up from PICU. One evening, I returned to Matthew's room to find my bed made up, the hospital blanket turned down, and a piece of Dove chocolate on my pillow. I walked out to the nurses' station to express my appreciation.

"Someone made up my bed for me, and there's a chocolate on my pillow! That's so kind and thoughtful! Thank you!" I said. One of the nursing assistants smiled sheepishly and made eye contact.

"You've been here almost ten days without a decent night's sleep. You haven't left him. You tend to him so well, so tenderly. You need some kindness. I will do what I can do," she said quietly. Tears glistened on her lashes; tears stung my eyes as well. I thanked her again and returned to the room. As I lay for another night in the hospital, I gazed up at the dark sky and thanked my Jesus for that woman's kindness. She saw my exhaustion, and my labor of love for Matthew. Moreover, my Jesus saw it. Even though I often felt like no one saw or cared, in His Word He said that He sees it all—nothing misses His notice. Though my day-to-day reality felt very different, by faith I tightly gripped the truth of Scripture for it was true no matter how unseen and forgotten I often felt.

The doctor made rounds between 7:00 and 7:30 AM, and I wanted to be up, dressed, and ready to talk coherently with him. The doctor and his gaggle of medical students moved from room to room on the unit, and I gauged their movements and timed out how long I had to get dressed and grab my first cup of coffee from the elevator lobby. Following his discussion with the medical students, he would slip in to examine Matthew, go back and talk with his students, and then speak with me about Matthew's progress and his concerns. He wanted Matthew to walk as much as possible, so we tried our best. Matthew also seemed determined to walk, and he and I were quite a spectacle. I gathered his tubes, wires, and IV pole, and steadied him. He trudged forward in his awkward, side-leaning gait, eyes wild, arms flailing as he huffed and puffed around the unit and up and down the hall.

Within the week, his chest X-rays improved, and the doctors began another discussion with me. Matthew needed a tummy tube for ease of adding nutrition and medication. It was a simple surgery that could be done as he recovered. The benefits would be that he could receive his seizure medication through the tube rather than by mouth. I could add extra hydration and nutrition through the tube, plus he could still eat by mouth as long as his food was pureed. I agreed, and he was put on the surgery schedule for the next day. A nurse from the GI department would stop by Matthew's room to show me how to use and change his tummy tube. Hospital staff suggested I stay in his room on the nursing floor as he would be back with his tummy tube in place in no time. I agreed, the same-day surgery crew wheeled him out and I settled in for the wait. I made a cup of coffee in the elevator lobby and went back to Matthew's room to send email updates and texts. I finished, and was thinking about a second cup of coffee when a nurse popped in; same-day surgery was bringing Matthew back up to the room. "That was fast!" I said. She laughed, "Yes, that is a quick surgery. He's almost done in recovery, then they'll bring him up," she said, and was gone.

A team of nurses in brightly colored scrubs wheeled a hospital bed into the pod and stopped at the nurses' station. "Matthew, from same-day surgery?" she said. Our nurse pointed to our room, I stood in the doorway and waved them in. Matthew was lying on the hospital bed, sedated, but waking up. The nurses transferred him onto the hospital bed in his room. One of them lifted Matthew's gown proudly, showing me his new hardware—a white plastic gadget that was attached to his tummy. Clear plastic tubing was attached to the gadget. The nurse clicked a button and gave the clear tubing a half-twist; it lifted off the white plastic gadget. She showed me several more times, clicking the button and doing the half-twist.

"See, it's nothing. Got it Mom?" she smiled. My head swam. I did not have it. "A nurse from GI will be up this afternoon to show you how to change the tubing and the whole thing," she said, pointing to the white gadget affixed to Matthew's tummy. "You handle hard things all the time, so this will be no problem," she said. I was unconvinced.

The same-day surgery crew left. I lifted Matthew's gown again. I clicked the button and gave the tubing the half-twist as the nurse had done. The tube detached and reattached easily from the white gadget. I could do that part; I took a deep breath. "One thing at a time," I told myself. "One thing at a time."

Matthew slept soundly. I sat in the blue recliner with an un-settled knot in my gut. The tummy tube added one more heavy re-sponsibility to my plate, which was already full. How would I learn to use this new gadget with ease? Change the whole thing? What if I screwed it up or hurt him? Questions raced one over the other through my mind. Our life had taken another downturn with the placement of a simple tummy tube. In some ways it would make life easier; in other ways, it meant we had just taken a major step on a downward trajectory.

"Lord? This feels like too much. Do I get to say that? I feel like I'm going to crack, but I don't get to do that. Hold me together. Help me be strong and do what I must do for Matthew," I prayed. There was only silence and the unsettled knot in my gut. I sat qui-etly in the blue recliner. Our nurse came and went, and then she spoke.

"Mom, you doing okay? You're very quiet," she said. I nodded; I didn't know what to say. Tears were already welling in my eyes and spilling onto my shirt. I swiped them away and moved to Mat-thew's bedside watching as she hung a bag of milky substance on his IV pole, and released a clamp on the tubing allowing it to flow into his tummy tube. "High-protein shake," she said as I flashed a questioning look in her direction. It looked easy; I could do that.

"I'll be back in when that's done. I'll show you how to unhook it," she said, and was gone. I sank into the blue recliner once again. I knew there was no way around this next hard thing in our jour-ney. I would have to keep plodding ahead, doing the next thing He asked of me, and then moving on to the next. I already knew the answer to my earlier question. It was a heavy load I carried, and I could say whatever I needed to say to my Heavenly Father—even when it felt like too much. I was not going to crack under the pressure because His everlasting arms held me up. The addition of the tummy tube, and whatever that meant for our trajectory was in His hands. I would continue to be in the fray, but I would be fine. For the moment, I could sit in the blue recliner and let the wordless groaning of my soul rise to Him, as I slumped, battle-weary against His chest.

The timer beeped on Matthew's bag, and our nurse returned. She walked me through how to unhook it and let me do it. It was easy; I could do that. She readied a round of Matthew's seizure medications and prepared to give them through his tummy tube. I watched her intently; I could do that. She recommended that Matthew rest well through the night. She could have the GI nurse come the next day to show me how to change the tubing and the device at home. I nodded and secretly welcomed the delay.

"He's been through a lot, Mom," she said. "You've also been through a lot. He's doing well and should be able to go home within a day or so—I hope he doesn't develop an ileus after surgery. Some kids do. That's no fun!" She was gone. "Ileus? Never heard of it," I thought as I stretched the sheets over the couch cushions to make up my bed for another night in the hospital.

The following day, Matthew was more wakeful, so the GI nurse paid her visit. She lifted Matthew's gown and walked me through the same clicking and half-twist steps the other nurses had shown me. Our nurse came and went. The GI nurse prepared to show me how to change the entire white plastic gadget. She detached the white plastic gadget and slid it off the tubing protruding from Matthew's tummy. There was a perfectly round hole in Matthew's abdomen the size of a hole-puncher. Wet stomach goop dampened his skin where the plastic gadget had been, and greenish stomach goop washed into the clear tubing. My head began to swim. The nurse was talking; my gut clenched; the nurse talked on. My throat was suddenly watery; I eyed the distance to the bathroom door. "This is where I tap out, Lord," I prayed. I jolted myself back.

"So, you think you've got that, Mom?" the nurse asked. I stared.

"The school nurse can help me, right?" I asked. The GI nurse looked confused and cast our nurse a questioning glance. Our nurse smiled and assured her it would be okay. The GI nurse packed up and left. I walked to the elevator lobby for a cup of ice water, returned to Matthew's room, and sank into the blue recliner. The following day, talk began among the nursing staff of Matthew being released. Our nurse agreed to expedite the paperwork. Then she brought up the term "ileus" she'd mentioned before.

"I'm concerned Matthew is in danger of developing an ileus. He hasn't had a bowel movement since his surgery, and that could be why," she said. "If that happens once you're home, you'll need to come back through the ER and be hospitalized for treatment. It is not uncommon, but does require a separate hospitalization." She brought me an information sheet explaining an ileus and treatment. As I packed up the room to go home, I folded the information sheet neatly and tucked it into an easily retrievable place in my purse; according to our nurse, I would likely need it.

As I unpacked at home, I read the ileus information sheet and laid it on the kitchen table. An ileus, it seemed, was an intestinal blockage that frequently happened following surgery. We were home a day before Matthew had a bowel movement. It was diarrhea. I read the information sheet over several more times. I needed to know exactly when to return him to the emergency room. His bowel blow-outs continued; he slept in snatches, and when he wasn't sleeping he just lay on his bedroom floor. I re-packed my hospital bag.

Late in the evening on Day Two, he began rolling back and forth and moaning. I called the on-call nurse in the emergency room and told her I was bringing him in. I woke Mark enough to let him know what was happening, loaded Matthew into the van, and went to the emergency room again. We were quickly moved into a side room. I referenced our recent hospitalization and surgery. Once again, things moved quickly. A doctor ordered abdominal imaging and I lugged Matthew down the hallway as before, stood him against the metal stand, wore the heavy black apron, and carried him back to the room. The imaging came back quickly and showed a substantial ileus.

We were immediately moved to a room on a nursing floor where we had never been before. I wheeled the transport wagon near the couch and gazed out at the blackness and a flat rooftop, punctuated by multicolored lights. "That's the helipad for the Life Flight helicopter. Kinda cool!" One of the nurses answered my unasked question. The doctor talked quietly to the nurses; the nurses knew the drill and sprang into action.

"He's got a tummy tube! Cool, that makes things way easier!" the nurse said as he settled Matthew in and assessed the situation. The doctor nodded and agreed.

I was used to caring for Matthew, and it was my M.O. during his hospitalizations to work alongside the nurses as appropriate. I stood beside Matthew's bed, gloved up, and started to help with a diaper change. It seemed my brain operated in slow motion. I tried to focus on the task before me and move through, step by step. My old strategy did not work. I felt myself wobbling and pressed my hip bone hard into the side of Matthew's hospital bed to steady myself. I could feel the nurses' gaze upon me.

"When did you last sleep?" he asked. I shrugged my shoulders; I didn't know the answer. I mentioned the events of the past two days, and three weeks prior. I struggled on. My hands would not do what my brain told them to do.

Matthew's nurse turned to me and made direct eye contact. "We've got this; you're exhausted," he said. "He's in good hands. Sit down." He steered me into the teal recliner behind me. I slumped sideways as voices faded around me.

"How we doin' in here?" My eyes fluttered open. Matthew's doctor stood beside his bed talking with the nurse. The nurse reported, I listened. It seemed Matthew was about halfway through the treatment process. I wondered what time it was; it was light outside. A hospital blanket covered me. The doctor nodded in my direction as she talked with the nurse with a questioning look.

"What's going on there? She okay? She's been there the whole shift," she said. The nurse nodded knowingly; the other nurse nodded affirmatively.

"She was exhausted. I made her sit down, she's been asleep sideways in that chair my whole shift," he said. The doctor grimaced sadly and shook her head, and she was gone.

"Would you be more comfortable on the couch?" a nurse asked me. I nodded numbly, and moved, bringing the hospital blanket with me. I lay down and was sinking again, powerless against the pull.

"Should we wake her?" a nurse asked her co-worker. I sat up, blinking away the fog. "We're leaving, it's the end of our shift. I wanted to be sure you were okay and that you got something to eat. You can order from food service. Matthew can't eat by mouth until tomorrow," she said. I nodded and thanked her for her kindness.

She smiled sadly, and said, "You needed that sleep; you were asleep in that chair when I got here this morning, and now it's time for me to leave." I looked out the window, it was dark. I thanked her again, and she was gone. I struggled to shake the brain fog. I had been asleep for more than an entire eight-hour work shift. Once again, I was the recipient of amazing kindness from strangers. I thanked God for them and their acts of tender service to me.

I roused myself and checked on Matthew. He slept soundly; I found the food service menu and placed an order. The new team of nurses came and introduced themselves. I walked around the unit, found the coffee machine, and returned with my steaming cup. A free evening stretched before me. Granted, I was in the hospital with Matthew, but the simple joys of coffee, a warm meal from food service, and minimal caregiving demands made it a pleasant prospect.

As I sat in the teal recliner eating my supper on the rolling hospital table, I marveled at the nurses' kindness. They had seen my exhaustion and cared enough to make me stop working. There was an opportunity for much-needed sleep, and they made me take it. I would have pressed onward in my exhaustion until I collapsed. I was used to pushing myself further and further because I had no other choice. I treasured their attention and kindness and thanked God for it. My commitment to Matthew's care was noticed. I was noticed and cared for.

Matthew improved, and by the next day he was eating by mouth, and his digestive tract was online again. Within days we returned home, but several new realities were settling heavily upon me. Though Matthew's tummy tube was a matter of convenience that made his care easier, it symbolized something else to me. We had taken a downward step. The reality of it all landed heavily upon me. I felt like I was being slowly squeezed by a massive vise. I was hard-pressed, but could honestly say, I was not forsaken. I talked to my Jesus all day and well into the night; He was with me as my circumstances pressed in hard. I was beaten up and worn out in the battle, but I was fighting on in His strength. Though I was often discouraged, His Word lifted my gaze toward eternity and our blessed hope—a promise resting securely upon the character of One Who promised—The Ancient of Days Who stooped to walk with me.

FOOD FOR THOUGHT:

1. Do you ever feel like your life circumstances are threatening to swallow you? Do they taunt and intimidate you with lies? What lies are they telling you? The truth of Scripture remains true no matter what lies the enemy hisses in our ears. What Scriptures would counter the lies the evil one is telling you?

2. I often felt the heaviness of discouragement and the truth seemed far away—like something for a sunny Sunday morning, not for the darkness and heaviness I felt. The truth *is* for that looming circumstance staring you down right now. He may seem far away and disinterested, but He is neither. Whatever you are feeling now, you can say to Him in raw and honest prayer.

CHAPTER 10

BLACK WATER AHEAD; PREPARE FOR CROSSING

"When you pass through the waters, I will be with you; and through the rivers, they shall not overwhelm you; when you walk through the fire you shall not be burned, and the flame shall not consume you."

Isaiah 43:2, ESV

"I am feeble and crushed; I groan because of the tumult of my heart. O Lord, all my longing is before you; my sighing is not hidden from you. My heart throbs; my strength fails me, and the light of my eyes—it also has gone from me."

Psalm 38:8-10, ESV

arly in 2012, when the boys were eleven, we were approved for a new seizure medication called ONFI. According to our neurology team, it worked wonders on seizures like Matthew's. We started Matthew on ONFI and within a few weeks his seizures were more controlled, although he still had them daily.

One afternoon I received a phone call from my process coordinator at the Regional Center. She reminded me that I had applied for funding for adaptive equipment months ago. Frankly, I had forgotten about it. Her call was to inform me that our funding was approved. There were ample funds to purchase both an adaptive car seat and a bath chair for Matthew. I requested recommendations from his school therapists on the best designs and quickly placed my order. The new equipment arrived within days. I could now safely bathe Matthew without the fear of a head injury in the shower.

I continued to work half days as a paraprofessional at our local special needs preschool. Luke was a fifth grader and a first-year Scout. My church friend Cynthia came faithfully each Monday evening so I could take Luke to his Scout meeting. She and Matthew became sweet friends as she cared for him with skill and kindness.

The school year ended, and Luke was off to church Family Camp at the lake with Cynthia and her family. As usual, he returned bronzed by the sun, worn out, miffed that camp was over, and yet thrilled at the prospect of the summer ahead. He was excited about his first year of Scout camp and the monthly campouts scouting offered. He was in his element as a Scout, making friends, and coming into his own as an adolescent.

Matthew's summer kicked off with half-day summer school, four days per week. Early each morning, I slipped into his room and ran a protein shake through his tummy tube and into his belly, followed by his seizure medications. I often diapered and dressed him as he slept, and became adept at slipping on the bus harness as he slept as well. When the bus came, I often carried him to the bus half asleep. The bus driver indicated he was often fully awake by the time they arrived at school. Once home, I took him to his room for a diaper change. He would often lie on his bed rolling around and giggling as I emptied his backpack and read notes from his teacher. One afternoon, Matthew was rolling on his bed as usual as I sorted through his backpack. Suddenly, he stopped, laid back against his pillow, and said, "Umma!" I turned, startled to see who was talking, he said it again: "Umma, I "uve" you!" I laughed out loud!

"I love you too, Matthew!" I said. He grinned. Luke was suddenly at Matthew's doorway. "Did he say he loved you, Mom?" he asked. "I thought I heard him. I wondered who said it." We marveled together and sat on Matthew's bed with him praising him for talking as we tried to encourage more speech. Matthew just grinned elfishly looking from Luke to me. Clearly, he'd said his piece, and was done. If he only had one sentence to say, I rejoiced that it was that one.

The last day of summer school was typically a water play day. It was Matthew's favorite day. As usual, I packed his swim trunks, towel, and a change of clothes. Paras at Matthew's school usually took pictures of the kids playing in the water and sent them home on the last day. Following water day at school, Matthew was typically exhausted and took a long nap after lunch. Matthew's bus came as normal and he was truly ready for lunch and nap. With Mark and Luke done with lunch and Mark headed off to work, I had a few precious moments of quietness to unpack Matthew's backpack and handle the papers, wet clothes, and crafts. I tossed the wet clothes into the laundry and sorted through the papers and crafts. Tucked into the pocket of Matthew's take-home folder was an envelope of photos from Water Day. In one photo Matthew was dancing and twirling in the spray of a rainbow-maker sprinkler in a golden splash of sunlight–he was dancing on a rainbow on a spray of gold. Tears stung my eyes. Scripture spoke of the rainbows that surround God's throne; I couldn't shake the image. I flipped to the next photo. Matthew stood on the school playground in his gait trainer, again, there was a splash of sunshine under his feet illuminating the pavement and his shoes in a golden glow—golden shoes, golden pavement. I blinked away the tears. "Yes Baby," I mused, "You'll know all about those golden streets and rainbows around God's throne!" I tucked the envelope into a protected corner of the kitchen cupboard and went about my day, but returned to them several times throughout the afternoon, and the summer. It seemed like a glimpse over the horizon. I tucked the thought away in a quiet corner of my mind for safekeeping.

I felt our life was at the mercy of a massive river. In our small boat, we were being dragged along in a powerful current. It was futile to fight the current or the river. However, we rested in the Hands of the Maker of the river. He was well aware of our plight, yet the current continued to pull us downstream toward a massive waterfall thundering in the distance. The Maker had been our Guide and Protector our entire journey, and He would be in the days ahead. As I stood there at the kitchen counter flipping through the pictures of Matthew's water day photos, I could feel the river's current beneath me gaining speed. Trepidation rose within me, yet I knew my Jesus would hold us fast as we hurtled toward the crashing falls, and the day we plummeted over the edge into the foaming abyss below.

With summer school in the rearview mirror, a long summer stretched before us, one of just being home together and mostly confined to the main living space of our house. It was an unusually hot summer with temperatures in triple digits almost daily. Given Matthew's lack of safety awareness and frequent seizures, I had to be always within arms' length of him. During these long summer days, there was nothing else I could do but hang out with him in our living room. The TV provided some distraction; Matthew mostly just wanted me to sing for him, and I gladly obliged.

Hymns were my old friends, and as I was always singing hymns for Matthew, it seemed fitting I should do so now. He enjoyed it and I did as well. I sang hymn after hymn, once again praying them over him as I did since he was a baby. He would often plop in my lap and peer curiously into my mouth as I sang as if asking, "How do you do that?" He would giggle as I stopped and started the sound to pique his curiosity. One hymn that became his favorite during that summer was "I'll Fly Away." When I sang it, he would often try to sing along, yelling and laughing at the same time. He would run around the living room hollering, laughing, and waving his arms as I sang. Often, I could barely sing, as choking sobs welled up and tears flowed as I laughed over his joyful noises. My heart broke afresh, knowing his release would most likely come as he "flew away" to heaven.

It was the summer of doing the truly important–the eternal, because Matthew wouldn't always be here. I wanted to have no regrets. I didn't want to wish I had spent more time singing the songs, holding him, memorizing the softness of his hair, the fall of his long dark lashes, and his dark brown eyes. Temporarily, things like laundry and dishes could wait; these were the days when heaven touched the earth. My hymns and songs opened heaven's portals illuminating the drudgery with the glow of our blessed hope.

Outside our tall windows, hummingbirds hovered and darted about the feeder like tiny glistening jewels. Large yellow or orange butterflies danced among the flowers—sometimes there was a dazzling blue one. Each glittering hummingbird and every flitting butterfly spoke of His tender care. For He spoke in His Word of His care for sparrows, and I knew He was well aware of Matthew and me spending another summer afternoon marveling at His creation and singing His praises. I did notice that He had forced me to slow down and simply be with Matthew. On one hand, there was nothing else to do, on the other, it seemed He was telling me, this was the important thing. The other things could wait.

Despite my earlier misgivings surrounding Matthew's tummy tube, I embraced it as an easy way to slip in his meds and extra nutrition. Once I got over my initial trepidation, I was able to give him meds and add in a protein shake with ease. I wondered to myself why I hadn't done it sooner as it helped so much. However, it was also an ever-present reminder of where we were on our journey. I had no way of knowing when or how our journey together would end, but I felt in the impending heaviness and whispers rose of the quiet recesses of my mind.

Summer waned into back-to-school preparations. Luke was making the massive leap from fifth grade to sixth. In our district, that meant he changed from the elementary school building to the middle school building. It was a much larger building with more students. He would be moving from room to room for various classes and have his own locker. I was certain Luke would be fine and would transition smoothly, but I also knew even if he were a flurry of nerves, he would not say so. Matthew's school started a few days before Luke's, and I counted on those days so I could get a few hours of reprieve to get Luke squared away for the leap to middle school.

Somewhere in the first few days of school, the ONFI stopped working. Matthew's seizures markedly increased. At the start of the school year, he also started getting sick, which also increased his seizure activity. With Matthew's increased illness and seizures, I was at home with him more than at school. It made the reality of me working outside the home seem increasingly ridiculous. Even though he was on several heavy medications, the seizures refused to stop. Something was wrong; his seizures were increasing rapidly. By mid-October, we were hospitalized once again, but home again for the boys' late October birthday. I baked a cake. I sang the birthday song, and we lit the candles for Luke to blow out for them both, as we usually did. I wheeled Matthew's wheelchair close to Luke's spot at the kitchen table and snapped a few photos, knowing it would likely be their last birthday together. The moment passed, yet neither boy understood what had just transpired. How could they? As I flipped through the pictures on my phone, the same heavy foreboding clenched my chest. I felt the pull of that proverbial river speeding up, dragging us more quickly downstream toward that thundering waterfall in the distance.

A few days after the boys' twelfth birthday, Matthew's seizures began steadily increasing. He seemed to be having one seizure after the other with little to no breaks between them. I carefully watched each seizure and its timing and logged them in my spiral notebook. I called the neurologist's nurse line, reported what I was seeing, and waited. I questioned if I was truly seeing what I thought I was seeing; if so, this was something I had never seen since he began having seizures at eighteen months old.

I re-packed my hospital bag and waited for the neurology nurse to call back. I was confident she would tell me to bring him in, so I began preparations for another hospital stay. I texted Mark telling him I was taking Matthew back to the emergency room, and asking him to be home by the time Luke's school was released. The neurology nurse called back; as expected, she said to bring him back through the ER. I stuffed my seizure log notebook into Matthew's backpack and loaded us up for another trip to the ER, and potentially another lengthy hospital stay.

Matthew and I were ushered into an exam room. A very young and unfamiliar doctor asked me the familiar questions and examined Matthew as usual. When I mentioned the frequency of his seizures, she eyed me skeptically. I mentioned our long history in the neurology clinic, his meds, my recent call to the neurology nurse line, and her recommendation that I bring him to the ER. Matthew continued to seize at the same rate he had been seizing at home, and I pointed that out to her; again she was skeptical. She excused herself, saying she would be back. She returned with an even younger-looking medical student carrying a notebook and a pen. She instructed him to log the seizures I reported to him, as he observed. He rolled his stool next to the exam table where Matthew lay, and we began.

"Here's one starting," I said, "lasting fifty seconds, grand mal." He wrote slowly. "Here's another," I said, "lasting 62 seconds, grand mal." He continued writing; Matthew's seizures continued and I continued reporting to him.

He stopped writing and eyed me skeptically. "You do know what seizures look like, right? Have you ever seen one before? Has he ever had them before?" he asked.

Ire rose within me like a smoldering inferno. I sucked in a massive breath through my nose and blew it out slowly through my mouth, holding eye contact with him as I did so. "Yes, I know what seizures look like. I've seen them many times; he's been having seizures since he was eighteen months old," I answered.

He looked at Matthew and at his notebook, as I continued to report. "Then, he's having constant seizures right now..." he said, and his voice trailed off.

I nodded, "Yes, sir," I said. "That is why we're here. That is why the neurology nurse sent us back to the ER. You may call neurology and speak to our neurologist or his nurse if you have questions." He nodded, excused himself, and said he'd be back; he was talking to the young doctor at the nurse's station. Within minutes they returned with a neurologist from the ER. He immediately recognized Matthew and me, prescribed sedation, and arranged for admittance to our regular floor. As the sedation took hold, Matthew's seizures slowed and he was out. I waited beside his gurney once again for someone to escort us up to his room. A pair of nurses came and wheeled Matthew and his gurney onto the transport elevator. I followed as usual, lugging our gear; the nurses settled Matthew in as usual. I dropped our bags on the couch, backed out of the way, and texted Mark an update.

It was midafternoon, and he was home from work, and Luke was home from school. Mark gave Luke the phone: "Hey Buddy," I said, "Brother and I are back at the hospital. That's why Daddy is there. We'll be here for a little while. Daddy will stay with you. I love you and will stay in touch." He handed the phone back to Mark; it was business as usual for Luke.

I settled in for another evening in a hospital room, except this time felt far different than others. His seizures were constant with no break in between. I stood beside Matthew's hospital bed with a sick, heavy knot in my gut. We were in uncharted waters; we were hurtling toward that thundering waterfall.

"Lord, this isn't good. We've never been here before. You know what's happening; please give me wisdom; hold onto us for whatever happens next," I prayed.

The nurses suggested that I order a meal from food service and try to eat. I had no interest but was hopeful Matthew would wake up, be hungry, and eat well, so I ordered for him. As his sedation wore off, he was awake enough to eat and did eat the meal that food service sent, and I was grateful. With his increased wakefulness, his seizures returned at the same rate—they were constant. I called in a nurse to observe and verify what I was seeing. She brought me a notebook and pen and asked me to keep a log for the doctor. I began again, marking the time, duration, and type of seizure, barely finishing one notation before starting the next. Our nurse came and went, reading my log and watching Matthew intently.

"He's having constant seizures. What you're writing is exactly what is happening here," she said. "I'm calling a doctor," I thanked her for taking notice of our perilous situation.

The neurologist from the ER returned and prescribed more sedation, saying he'd confer with the neurology team in the morning, and make a game plan. Our regular neurologist would come to see us in the morning. The further sedation took hold and once again, Matthew was out. There was nothing left to do but make up my bed once again on the hospital couch, staring up at the night sky through the hospital window, talking to my Jesus as I drifted off to sleep and tears slipped into my ears.

Mark needed to return to work, and we needed somewhere for Luke to stay. One of our neighborhood friends volunteered for Luke to stay at her house while Matthew was in the hospital. Luke and her son were friends and classmates as well as Scout friends. I agreed and was thankful for her help and kindness, but felt the need to talk with Luke. I called the office at Luke's school, explained our situation, and asked if I could talk with Luke. The secretary was glad to call Luke out of class to talk with me. I explained that he should walk home with his friend, and gave him a vague update on Matthew. He was concerned for Matthew but also excited to stay with his friend. I was relieved that Luke was in good hands and wouldn't miss school.

It was mid-morning when our neurologist came; a somber air hung about him as he examined Matthew. Then he pulled up a chair to talk with me. They had already prescribed all the appropriate seizure control medications and adjusted the dosages. There were no further medications to try.

"What about ONFI? It was working well, and then it stopped," I said.

"Yes, that's what we're finding with ONFI. It was so new when Matthew started it that we didn't know. We're finding it buys us another six months. After six months, it stops working, it seems," he said. He smiled sadly.

"This is what we didn't want to happen. He's having constant seizures—Matthew is in status," he said. "There is one more option; admission to the PICU is required. He would have to be intubated. It's a medically induced coma, essentially to reboot the brain in hopes that the seizures would slow or dissipate as he wakes up—then palliative care…" his voice trailed off, "…hospice. The neurology team will confer later this morning, make recommendations, and get back to you." He went silent, staring at the floor, then raised his eyes to mine, a sad and silent "I'm so sorry" and "I don't know what to do" passed silently between us. I nodded numbly. He rose and was gone.

This was the moment I had dreaded for years. I thought it would feel different; perhaps there would be rushing winds, the inexplicable intervention of angelic doctors or nurses, doves, or goosebumps. There was none of that.

There in a hospital room, on a gloomy Thursday morning in November, our tiny boat spun wildly into the speeding current toward the sheer drop-off of the dreaded thundering waterfall. Icy black water soaked me as we spun helplessly in the thick gray mist. We were falling. I was screaming inside—my soul screams lost in the roar of the waterfall. We were hurtling downward in slow motion, it seemed. Icy white-grey foam swallowed us, I was sinking, reeling, spinning—plummeting downward in the thundering, icy grayness. Then there was silence.

Like many times before, I was alone with Matthew in a hospital room, but this time was different. I stood beside Matthew's hospital bed staring down at him. He lay motionless under heavy sedation. I was shaken... numb. My mind swirled. My stomach dropped with a dull thud. In my heart, I had known this day would come. Matthew had always been in God's hands from eternity past; the same was true now. This Jesus, who had become my strength and song through countless desperate night watches, would again prove Himself faithful. Where Jesus led, I would follow. Wherever He was, we would be too.

I wrote an email update to our family and church friends, explained the procedure as best as I could, requested prayers, and hit "send." Within the hour, my brother-in-law showed up to sit with me through his lunch hour. As he returned to work, the neurologist arrived. The neurology team had conferred; the medically induced coma was a go. They would transfer Matthew to PICU as soon as a unit was available and begin the procedure. My stomach flipped, and my heart sank with a dull thud. Nurses came and went, I stood stock-still beside Matthew's bed. I couldn't think or move. There was a tap on the door; it was my church friend, Misty. She'd read my email and come to be with me. She came to me; I burst into tears. She held me as I sobbed; I struggled to catch my breath. She made me sit in the recliner behind me and lower my head. She coaxed me to breathe in and out. I was trembling. I began to catch my breath, and my trembling slowed. I sat in the recliner simply breathing in and out. A nurse tapped on the door, they were ready to move Matthew to the PICU. I backed out of the way as several nurses filled the room. I gathered our gear and waited.

"You can go back to work," I said to Misty.

She shook her head, "No, I'm not leaving you like this; not now."

The nurses gave the signal and we were on the move. We crowded into the transport elevator, someone clicked a series of buttons on the panel, and we were plunging downward to PICU once again. The elevator bumped to a stop, and the door opened once again into the sunlit, beige hallway. The nurses wheeled Matthew into the same glassed-in unit. The nurse approached with the same suggestion that we wait in the waiting room. She scanned her badge, and the same double doors swung open. Then, we were back in the same waiting room. The waiting room was full, but we found an empty bench along the wall and sat down. There was nothing to say, there was nothing to do but wait, so we waited.

"Matthew's mom?" It was the receptionist. "They're ready for you," she said, swiping her badge as the double doors swung open. Misty and I walked into Matthew's unit. I was stunned. He was barely visible. A massive device nearly covered his face; his chest moved up and down. The machine was breathing for him. His head was wrapped in the familiar gauze turban he'd worn during his many EEGs. The same probes were glued to his head, the wires dangling from the opening in the top of the turban snaked to the monitor behind his bed. His legs were encased in the same compression devices, an IV pole stood on his right with several vials of medication dripping down the clear tubing and into the port in his arm. I gripped his silver bed railing and stared at the reality before me. Misty's arm was around my shoulder. I glanced around the room and spied my old friend, the green recliner rolled into the corner. I asked the nurse if I could retrieve it. She nodded. Misty and I maneuvered it into an unobtrusive place; I stowed my gear beside it.

It was time for Misty to return to work, so I walked her to the elevator lobby, hugged her, and thanked her for staying with me. She stepped on the elevator, the door closed, and she was gone. There was nothing left to do except return to Matthew's unit. My old friend waited, and though this time was far different than other PICU stays, I did what I had done other times. I returned to the green recliner and waited—waiting for what, I was unsure. I texted Mark an update. My head thumped, my stomach growled, and my eyes burned. I leaned my head back, closed my eyes, and let the dinging monitors and whooshing of the compression devices drift away. The pinging monitors jolted me awake; the nurse had covered me with a hospital blanket. I thanked her.

She reminded me to reserve a space in the Ronald McDonald Parent Rooms, so once again, I walked the beige hallway and turned in at the familiar sign. I received my room assignment and keys and stowed my bags in the room. I was back, but so much was different. I stretched out on the bed and let the heart cries I could not articulate rise to heaven. Tears streamed, sobs shook my body, screams spewed from me. My body curled into the fetal position. I heard myself praying through screaming sobs: "Lord, Matthew—PICU again? This is bad, this is different. Palliative care—hospice? He's dying, he's dying! Lord, what?!" My breath came in short, heaving gasps. There was a knock at the door. I sat up on the bed and forced myself to breathe in, and then out. I opened the door. The receptionist stood there with a questioning look. "Are you okay?" she asked; I nodded.

"My son is in PICU. It's not good," I explained. She nodded and returned to her desk. I clicked the door shut, regrouped, and returned to Matthew's unit.

Later that evening, two of my sisters came to visit, but before they left, they requested we pray. In the dimly lit waiting room, we pulled our chairs together and cried out to the God of Heaven. Our tears flowed. My sisters held me as I prayed with heaving sobs. As they held me, I heard myself repeatedly praying, "No God, not my baby! Please no, not my baby!" We said our "amens," and my sisters left. Following that prayer time, an image dropped into my mind. Jesus stood with His hand outstretched over an expanse of churning, black water. He wordlessly beckoned me to follow. I knew what He meant. He wanted my absolute trust as He took Matthew home. His silent promise: "…when you pass through the waters, I will be with you…"

Heartsick and physically ill from the grim reality ahead, I took up my post in the green vinyl recliner in the corner of Matthew's unit. As I settled into my PICU routine, the headache that was with me when we came to the PICU settled in for an extended stay, morphing into a full-blown migraine. I found a few bites of a bagel would stay down, allowing me to take my pain reliever; that pattern remained for days. An invisible hand, it seemed, clenched the back of my neck and the left side of my head. Each day seemed more nauseating than the last as doctors explained in brutally raw terms the end-of-life issues before me.

I signed a DNR. The palliative care nurse ushered me into a small room adjacent to the PICU furnished with a couch, a table, and a few armchairs. It seemed the sort of room where end-of-life talk happened. The palliative care nurse and I talked about where we would like Matthew to pass—at the hospital, a hospice house, or at home.

Luke continued to stay with our neighborhood friends. Mark continued to work as much as possible. On a gloomy November afternoon, I tucked myself into a window seat in the Ronald McDonald Parent Room, gazing out at the damp tar paper roof and the glossy blackbirds loitering about as I dialed Mark. We needed to talk about serious things. He picked up; I gave him a brief update on Matthew. I mentioned my serious conversations with doctors and the hospice team. I relayed our frank conversations.

"We need to break this to Luke. He needs to know this isn't like all the other hospitalizations," I said. "When we do that, we need to ask him where he thinks Matthew should pass—in the hospital, a hospice house, or at home. He may be freaked out with Matthew passing at home—some kids may be…" my voice trailed off. There was silence.

After a moment he said, "I was planning on coming down later today. I can bring Luke and we can tell him then," he said. I agreed.

"We also need to start thinking about a funeral—who you'd like to preach, where—all that…" again my voice trailed off. Mark mentioned our pastor as the obvious choice, and I agreed. We hung up. I sat for a long time in the window seat, the gloomy dampness outside mirrored the heaviness within me.

Later that afternoon Mark and Luke came to visit. I walked Mark and Luke into the same furnished conference room where the palliative care nurse and I had talked. Luke eyed me, then Mark; he sat on the couch beside Mark.

"Buddy, we need to talk about Matthew," I began, "I know he's been in the hospital a lot all along. We come home with more medicine and he does better for a while and then goes back." Luke nodded. "This time is very different. He's not going to make it, Buddy," I said, my tears spilling down my cheeks, I swiped them away with my sleeve. Luke stared at me dumbfounded.

"Matthew's gonna die?" he asked, his gaze shifting from Mark to me. I nodded. He doubled over, squeezing his eyes tightly shut, tucked his head into his elbows, pulling his hands over his head—

he was sobbing. I knelt on the floor in front of him, and he grasped for me, collapsing into me. His tears soaked into my sweatshirt, mine dripped into his hair. His sobs quieted, and we dried our eyes.

"One more question, Buddy," I said, "When Matthew passes, where do you think he should be? In the hospital? At a special hospice house or our house?" I asked.

Without hesitation, he said, "He would want to be at home. That's where he's comfortable—in his room with his family. That's the only right place." Mark and I nodded; it was decided. Mark and Luke went home. I settled in for another evening in the PICU.

I was reeling end over end in a sickening nightmare that was bearable only because of the kindness of church friends and family. Their well-wishes became compassion as their kindness showed up in tangible ways—a latte and a listening ear, a Panera salad and prayer, Advil, and open arms. Mostly friends came to listen, comfort me, and help shoulder my impossibly heavy burden. The loving-kindness of our Lord had shown itself once again as family and friends became the hands and feet of Jesus bringing comfort in unbearable circumstances. Matthew simply lay motionless in his coma, barely visible beneath the vent tubing, tangle of wires, and the bundle of EEG probes pasted to his head. The doctors scheduled a Care Conference for the day after Thanksgiving. In that meeting, we would discuss the next steps in Matthew's long-term care—it would become my personal Black Friday.

On Thanksgiving Day, my parents drove up to be with me. Local churches provided a Thanksgiving Day meal in the Ronald McDonald parent room, so we went. As I stood in the serving line waiting, a woman approached me. "You look like you're carrying the weight of the world on your shoulders," she said. I was taken aback. Was it that obvious?

"Yes ma'am," I said. "My son is in the PICU; he's dying." It shocked me to hear myself say it; it seemed more true to say it aloud. The woman patted my shoulder, said she'd pray for me, and moved on.

My parents and I filled our plates and found a table near the window. My parents chatted among themselves about the meal. I stared out the window at the flat wet rooftop.

"You need to eat," Mom said. "At least try some turkey, you need the protein."

I nodded, forking a piece of turkey and placing it in my mouth. I mushed it around in my mouth and forced myself to swallow it. It was all I could do. Mom brought me a slice of pumpkin pie, and again I tried. I couldn't do it. My parents stayed until midafternoon and left for home. Mom agreed to come up to be with me for the Care Conference the following day.

The PICU days became a week and Matthew's eyelids began to flutter, and his hands began to move. He was coming out of his coma. As he slowly came out of the coma, his seizures returned, but they were coming at ten per hour rather than continuously. The following morning, the entire team of PICU doctors, neurologists, and the palliative care team filed into the conference room near Matthew's unit. My mom and sister sat on one side of me, and Mark on the other. A sick knot lay heavily in my gut as the meeting began. Each team, in turn, gave their report. The neurologists deemed the procedure a moderate success and recommended plans to stabilize Matthew on a regular nursing floor. The others agreed. We would transition Matthew home on hospice. It was done, so clinically and matter-of-factly in a hospital conference room, and my life changed again. The doctors seemed relieved and filed out. A lone doctor remained at the table typing on his laptop. My head began to swim and my throat was suddenly wet. Doctors loitered in the doorway. I couldn't escape to the bathroom. Tears streamed as sobs burst from me, again my breath came in short, screaming bursts. I struggled to breathe. Mark stared at me, then grabbed the trash can. My mom and sister coaxed me to breathe in and out. The doctor looked up from his laptop and made a quick exit. Matthew's nurse peered in at us. As my breathing regulated, we all walked out to Matthew's unit, and my mom and sister prepared to leave. Mark and I walked them to the elevator lobby and they were gone. Mark went home shortly thereafter.

Later that afternoon, we wheeled Matthew with his necessary equipment from the PICU to a regular nursing floor. He was awake, but dopey and clearly unaware of his surroundings. He stared incredulously past me as I helped the nurses wheel him into the transport elevator. My friend Cynthia came to see us that evening. Cynthia and I stood at his bedside talking. Matthew's gaze rested upon me momentarily, and then full recognition flashed across his face. He grasped wildly for me, half laughing, half crying. Cynthia lifted him into my lap as I sank into the recliner behind me. He flung his arms around my neck, planted a wet, mushy kiss on my cheek, and said, "Umma! Umma!" Cynthia was crying; tears streamed down my cheeks, dripping from my chin and down my neck and soaking into my shirt, but I didn't care. Matthew's joy upon seeing me was evident. He had hugged me, kissed me, and said my name—he had said my name a few times before, but he had never initiated a hug and had never kissed me. He clung to me for a long time, then just sat in my lap, looking at me and smiling.

We began stabilizing on a regular nursing floor, and within days, he was sitting up in his wheelchair, eating, and attempting a few wobbly steps. He came back from his coma knowing how to give hugs, much to our delight, and was fond of giving them to

Luke and me. Early in December, we transitioned home on hospice. The transition came with an overwhelming medication schedule, orders for home health equipment, and private-duty nursing. Home health equipment invaded like unwelcome guests, a grim reminder of what hospice means. We arranged private duty nursing in a valiant effort to allow me a full night's sleep, something that had not been part of my reality for twelve years. Though Matthew had made remarkable progress, his brain and body were completely overloaded by his regimen of seizure meds, new caregivers, and his recent coma. For two weeks, he slept all day and he spent his nights yelling and reeling wildly as he tried in vain to stand. I often stayed up all night, assisting the nurses with Matthew's care, as it was more than they had bargained for. Most of the nurses stayed only one shift and never returned.

As some nurses left, others rose to the challenge and stayed. Matthew became more comfortable with them, as his body began to regulate. Late one evening, after our night nurse arrived, I was passing the torch to him as I got ready for bed. Our nurse checked on Matthew and settled at our kitchen table, charting on his laptop as I talked with him. I saw movement in the hallway. Matthew stood in the hallway wide-eyed. I silently pointed down the hallway, our nurse turned around stunned. "He did it! He worked at it until he relearned to walk!" he whispered. He eased into the hallway to both encourage Matthew and catch him if he fell. Matthew walked toward him slowly, his expression a mixture of confusion and amazement.

In the days that followed, Matthew seemed determined to walk as much as possible, but needed hands-on assistance. Mark seized the opportunity, supporting Matthew as they repeatedly walked the perimeter of the living room, dining room, foyer, and up and down the wall. Matthew's progress amazed the nurses, making hospice seem absurd. I met with school officials and arranged for him to return to school a few hours per day in the new semester. However, I knew it would never happen. The day arrived for Matthew's classroom Christmas party and I decided to take him. It would allow his teachers and paras the opportunity to see him and help him become reacquainted with familiar surroundings and people. He knew exactly where he was. Paras helped him onto his adaptive bike. He pushed the pedals a few rotations. Paras helped him get into his gait trainer, and he moved it a few steps. It was all he could do. However, it was truly amazing, considering where he'd been just weeks before. We gathered with his class for a group picture. I knew it was his final school trip. He seemed to know it, too. As we gathered up to leave, I tried to support him as he walked. He collapsed. He was done. I carried him to the van and drove home. The old sick knot dropped in my stomach with a thud.

We prepared for Christmas; it would be an odd sort of Christmas, but we would celebrate nonetheless. With Matthew in the care of nurses, Mark, Luke, and I made a few quick batches of Christmas candy. We took a chance, and put up the tree in the living room. I sent Mark Christmas shopping. My parents came for Christmas Day, bringing dinner and gifts with them. We celebrated quietly, knowingly. We were bracing for impact.

FOOD FOR THOUGHT:

1. When have you sensed God slowing you down, so you could see Him, feel Him, and be fully present for a season? What was the result? How did you feel? What did He show you?

2. When has God led you through deep difficulty that you thought would surely crush you? How did you survive it? What role did the Scripture play in that season?

CHAPTER 11

THE CROSSING

"My joy is gone; grief is upon me; my heart is sick within me."

Jeremiah 8:18, ESV

"Then Job arose and tore his robe and shaved his head and fell on the ground and worshiped. And he said, "Naked I came from my mother's womb, and naked shall I return. The Lord gave, and the Lord has taken away; blessed be the name of the Lord."

Job 1:20-21, ESV

After Christmas, Matthew began to regress. He could no longer stand, even with assistance, and he seemed to be in pain. Though the neurology team planned a surgery after New Year's to place a vagal nerve stimulator, it was obvious that he wasn't strong enough to survive another sedation. I knew the surgery would never happen. Nevertheless, I took Matthew to his pre-op appointment and met the hospice nurse at the appointment. The hospice nurse looked him over as we waited in the exam room, and immediately recognized what was happening. He had made his stellar comeback, but now his body was winding down. Matthew was dying.

She suggested I take him home and keep him comfortable. She would come for a visit later that afternoon. I did so, and when she arrived, we began oxygen and continued to keep him comfortable. I called my parents and suggested they come if they wanted to see Matthew again this side of eternity. The private duty nurse and I began an all-night vigil; a suffocating death pall settled over the house.

My parents decided to come and arrived later that morning. I tried to busy myself by preparing a meal for them, pushing through the pain to do what needed to be done, operating in what had become my *modus operandi* over the years. I worked alone in the kitchen, forcing myself through each step; tears streaming. My mother appeared in the doorway.

"What are you doing? Can I help you?" she asked.

"Making some lunch. We'll all need something to eat," I said. Mom's gaze rested on me, she shook her head sadly; my tears overtook me, and I was in her arms sobbing and screaming—she held me there.

Mark had made an appointment at the funeral parlor for after lunch. We needed to pick out Matthew's casket and make funeral arrangements and payments. My parents were there, so Mark and I went. I sat, ghost-like and numb throughout the appointment. Mark and the funeral director talked in hushed tones, asking me for my input at intervals. I nodded numbly in response, barely hearing or comprehending their words. Caskets were displayed around the room with suggested drapes and floral arrangements; it was a surreal experience. We drove home in silence; my tears streaming. My dad, Luke, and I sat beside Matthew's bed. We sang hymns, and he prayed for Matthew and our family. Mom and Dad left in late afternoon, to be home before dark. I promised to call Mom as soon as Matthew passed.

The afternoon droned on, and the hospice nurse suggested I lay down with Matthew and try to sleep. I was glad to try to snuggle beside him. As I did so, he sensed my presence, smiled and nestled his cheek against mine. I held his hand and drifted off to sleep. Later that evening, I touched base with our pastor and small group leader to keep them abreast of the situation and ask for ongoing prayers.

Mark suggested I try to catch another nap. He assured me that he would stay with Matthew, so I laid down on our bed and was out. The next thing I knew, Mark was shaking me awake and urging me to come. Matthew was fading, but the hospice nurse said I had time to shower and encouraged me to do so. I showered quickly, numbly. I talked to my Jesus as I did so, as I had done so many times before. He was silent. I simply felt His fixed, piercing gaze upon me. His hand remained extended over the choppy black waves–it was time to walk into that icy, dark water. My head pounded, and my stomach clenched into a knot, but with quiet resolve to follow Jesus into that churning black sea, I extended my trembling hand to His and stepped into the icy black waves.

I gathered Mark and Luke and my well-worn Bible and hymnbook. We settled down on Matthew's bed prepared to stay with him until he passed into eternity. How could we not be there when he needed us most? How could we miss such an awful, yet beautifully holy moment as Matthew's passing? So, there we were, holding his hands and walking with Matthew as far as we could toward Heaven's gate. Our tears flowed; I sang hymn after hymn for him and for us–the same hymns I had always sung for him. Time crept along as a gray pall crept slowly over his frail body. As he slipped away, he opened his eyes halfway, his clouded gaze rested momentarily on Luke and me. He closed his eyes, and within moments, passed into eternity. His battle was over!

A rush of relief, mingled with profound sadness and deep soul pain flooded me. Matthew was finally healed, whole, and free–the seizures had stopped! I could only feel relief and joy for him. The countless prayers I prayed for his healing were finally answered. While I blessed the Lord for Matthew's release, I was crushed by the loss. My soul wound was deep—as deep as the devotion with which I cared for him since he was born. I would never be the same again. At the same time, I knew this same Jesus, who had carried me through countless desperate days, would carry me through this profound loss. However, healing was a task for another day, now the wound was fresh and bleeding, and my soul was screaming in pain.

The hospice nurse began her documentation and called Matthew's doctors. She showed me how to dispose of Matthew's medications properly; we stood together in the dimly lit kitchen disposing of them one by one, grateful prayers of thanksgiving mingled with tears of brokenness as we did so. I called my mother; we talked quietly through our tears. I composed the email to friends and family and sent it out. We waited for the team from the funeral home to come for Matthew's body.

The hospice nurse urged me to go in and sit with his body alone for a few minutes. I walked across the threshold of his bedroom as I had many other times. His body lay still, his hands clasped over his chest as the hospice nurse had placed them. I touched his forehead; it was no longer warm with life. I fingered his soft brown hair and brushed my hand over his half-closed eyes. His dark brown eyes were fixed and empty, no longer seeing the pain of his earthly existence, yet now seeing the glories of heaven and the face of my beautiful Jesus. Brutal reality plunged its dagger deep into my soul. I collapsed over his corpse, heaving sobs wracked my body as hoarse screams poured from my wounded soul; I couldn't catch my breath. I forced myself to breathe in and out. As I sat on Matthew's bed beside his lifeless body, song lyrics drifted into my head and settled there, and I began to softly sing: *"Because He lives, I can face tomorrow. Because He lives, all fear is gone. Because I know He holds the future, then life is worth the living, just because He lives."* Because my Jesus lives, and Matthew was now healed and whole in His presence, I could rise again and move forward. He had been my strength and song through the entire uphill journey, He would be the same in the new journey ahead. I had done my best for Matthew in His strength. He was safely in the Savior's arms. There was nothing left to do but walk away. It was obvious that Matthew was no longer there; what remained was an empty shell. I rose and walked away, crushed, yet at perfect peace.

A solemn team in black arrived from the funeral home to re-trieve his body. The hospice nurse suggested that I may want to look away as they carried him out, but I refused. What was one more brutal sight after what I'd already experienced? Mark and I stood arm-in-arm as the team silently, solemnly, carried Matthew's corpse down the hallway. I could see the outline of his face un-der the sheet-draped gurney as they passed. I made myself look, unflinchingly, at the brutal reality. They passed through the front door and were gone into the winter night.

The hospice nurse left shortly thereafter, and we were left with a silent house and stark reality. I went to check on Luke, who, at 12 years old, had just watched his twin brother pass. He was shaken but okay. I stayed to talk with him and pray with him. I caught sight of myself in the bathroom mirror. My face was puffy and bright pink, and my swollen eyelids nearly enveloped my eyes; they peered out through puffy slits. I flipped off the light and slipped into bed. Mark and I lay side by side, silent and still. "What just happened to us?" I whispered up into the darkness. "I know," he said. We were both crying. Somewhere in the wee hours, I drifted to sleep.

I woke mid-morning the following day and lay numb and soul-sick as I gathered my thoughts. In the kitchen lay an array of medical equipment and tubing. In the corner of the dining room stood his empty blue wheelchair. Though all were reminders of the brutal reality that he was no longer here, they were also reminders pointing toward the more blessed and beautiful reality that Matthew was truly home, healed. He did not need tubing or his wheelchair now. It seemed irreverent to move any of it; it was too soon. I made coffee and sipped it quietly. Day One of my post-Matthew life had begun.

Mark and Luke got up, and we ate our breakfast in silence; a thick, heavy sadness hung about the kitchen table. There was nothing to say. Matthew's empty blue wheelchair stood at the end of the table in its regular space, a silent testament to his absence. After breakfast, Luke suggested that we all go together to walk our dog, Joey. The suggestion startled me; but there was no reason we couldn't now. I agreed. We looped on Joey's harness, bundled against the winter wind, and stepped out into the nipping cold. Thick, lacy frost clung to the naked tree branches and brown grass. Thin shells of ice covered the frozen puddles. We walked the trails in silence. My phone buzzed in my pocket. It was my friend Katherine.

"So, how are you? Dumb question, I know, but I wanted to check on you, friend," she said. I told her we were out walking our dog together because we could now. It was all strange, surreal, and overwhelmingly sad. We chatted and hung up. Mark, Luke, and I walked on in silence with Joey.

The days that followed were spent in funeral preparations and raw pain. We took clothes to the funeral home for Matthew to wear in his casket. We met with our pastor to finalize the service. The funeral date was set; it would be held in the chapel. We asked church friends to serve as Matthew's pallbearers. Our local paper came out. Matthew's obituary was listed among the others. Neighbors rang our doorbell and stood tearfully on the porch extending a platter of cold cuts or a casserole. Our community group at church began carrying in meals. We leafed through photos and sent them to the funeral home for a slideshow. We made photo displays for the table of mementos for the funeral day. We made trips to department stores to buy proper funeral clothes—Luke needed black pants and shoes, and Mark needed a shirt and tie. I needed a dress and went alone to find one. In my heaviness of soul, I felt the only appropriate attire would be the longest, most heavy black dress I could find. I trudged through one store after the other rifling through racks of post-holiday clearance items, finding nothing suitable.

"Lord, I just need a dress to wear to Matthew's funeral. Something nice enough to honor him," I prayed as I turned to make one last loop through the clearance racks. Hanging on the end of the rack I'd passed several times was a stylish black dress. It was the right size and was marked down to an outlandishly low price. I tried it on. It was as perfect as a funeral dress can be. I quickly bought it, silently thanking Him. I would wear it with a shimmering string of pearls and bracelet to remind myself of Heaven's gates and the dazzling beauty Matthew now beheld.

We prepared for the family coming into town for the funeral. A sister flew in, and other relatives drove from out of state. The stream of casseroles and platters of sandwiches was endless. The evening before Matthew's funeral was his visitation and private viewing. We invited family and church friends who had cared for him—my friend Cynthia, Ms. Pamela, his para from school, and our neighbor Teresa who had helped care for him since he was a baby. We dressed in our funeral clothes, drove to the funeral home, and filed into the funeral parlor. Matthew's casket stood open in the front of the room. Family clustered in the back of the room away from the uncomfortable reality. I grabbed Mark's hand and Luke's in the other and prepared to walk resolutely to Matthew's casket.

"You ready?" I asked them. They nodded. Together we walked up the aisle to Matthew's casket and peered inside. He lay with his hands folded over his stomach; he looked like a mannequin—a Matthew-like mannequin. I was heartbroken but with a settled peace. I was crushed, but knew I had done my absolute best for him, in God's strength. However, standing in the funeral parlor looking down at your son's lifeless body is not for the anemic of soul. Mark, Luke, and I stood there in silence, our hearts screaming with pain, yet it was as obvious then as it had been the moment he passed: Matthew was absent from his body and at home with the Lord.

We planned to host family and friends at our home following the private viewing, and everyone filed in. My sisters and church friends had prepared and arranged the bountiful array of deli trays, sandwich platters, and desserts from church and neighborhood friends into an ample feast. Family and friends gathered in our living room, enjoying one another's company while quietly acknowledging the reason for our gathering.

On the funeral day, we drove to the church as we'd done countless times, but this time was so different. As we entered the church, I saw a delivery cart parked outside the office, on the cart were funeral flowers marked "Matthew Romang-funeral." I'd seen similar floral arrangements in the same place many times bearing the names of others on the cards. This time, they were for us. What was a regular workday delivery for the church staff and florist, marked a monumental day of loss for someone–this time it was us.

We arranged the picture boards and laid out the mementos of his life—his favorite blue blanket, his well-worn crash helmet, and his favorite toys. We greeted friends and took our places in the receiving line. As I stood between Mark and Luke, I glanced over at the casket. To my surprise, the brand name on the casket said "Matthew's." How fitting. The visitation began, and friends and family streamed in. People we'd known from church since before the boys were born came with those who had been beside us the whole journey. Family from out of town, and family nearby joined the stream of mourners, too. Mark's co-workers and those from my school came, along with Matthew's teachers and therapists, and even his doctors. Our pastor preached Jesus's love and forgiveness. He spoke of comfort and peace from Psalm 121. Our friend sang "Untitled Hymn," the hymn I'd sung as Matthew passed into eternity. We all stood and sang out "I'll Fly Away!" It was only fitting we should do so.

The funeral was over, and we filed out, following Matthew's casket to the waiting hearse. We pulled our vehicle behind the hearse, joining the slow, solemn procession to the cemetery. At the graveside service, we settled into our folding chairs on the green astroturf mat, in the bright, bitter cold, and sat waiting. Our pastor read from Romans 8 and spoke a few words of comfort, reassurance, and truth. He prayed, and it was over. Family and friends filed past nodding gravely, smiling sadly, or sympathetically patting my shoulder as they passed. Mark and Luke filed past Matthew's casket and began walking up the hill toward the waiting cars. I stood before Matthew's casket alone. I froze. I placed my hand on his casket, as an immobilizing wave of grief flooded me. In life, I had never left Matthew anywhere unless I was certain he was safe. Now, for the first time in my life, I had to walk away and leave him there. Though I knew what lay in the casket was an empty shell, I was frozen, sobbing, and my knees giving way beside his casket. In my periphery, the funeral director hesitated in indecision, then inched closer as he saw me going down. "She needs help!" he called. Someone lifted me. Someone was holding me around my waist and walking me up the hill. Someone was saying, "Walk away, it's time to walk away! Come on, keep walking."

After the funeral dinner, we simply drove home to our strangely quiet house where I slumped on the couch and quickly fell asleep. I was jarred awake by the chiming doorbell. The funeral director stood on our porch. He solemnly handed me an array of funeral flowers that were left at the church. He smiled sadly and was gone. It was over.

Matthew's life had been a struggle from his first breath to his last. I could only feel relief and joy for him. Matthew's special needs were costly for me–exhaustion, helplessly watching as he suffered year after year, and the final tearing asunder of my very soul as he died. Yet, I bless the journey, for where else but in desperation would the Lord of All Creation stoop down to walk with me? Where else but in pain would the Suffering Servant carry my impossibly heavy load? Where else but in loneliness could I find such a Friend? Without the pain, I could have never known Jesus as I do, so I bless the journey, for by it, the Almighty One has become my strength. The Sovereign Lord has become my Peace and the Gentle Shepherd has become my Comfort, and the Healer of my broken heart.

With Matthew's funeral over, and friends and family back to work, a thick swirling fog descended upon my soul. Had I not cultivated life-giving dependence on God early in our journey, I would surely have become disoriented, plunging into the grayness, wildly grasping for the solid ground that lay beneath my feet. Despite the emotions that pulled me toward the fog, I sank into the solid rock of truth. There I was safe, despite the disorienting grayness that threatened to swallow me. There I stayed for innumerable days.

Matthew's journey was over, as was the journey he and I shared. Though he was healed and at home in heaven, I lay gravely wounded and bleeding out beneath the fog. A new journey lay before me, one of healing, hope, and restoration. Numbly, ghost-like, I rose to begin the journey, unsure of where, or even how to move forward or begin to heal while in such soul-pain.

Scripture speaks of seeds planted within the soil. In the cool, damp earth, that seed dies. Yet in its dying, it is transformed. What breaks through the soil as a tender green shoot is not the dry hard shell we placed into the earth. What bursts from the ground in the warm sunshine was encased within the seed, and released to the transformation process by its death. I could plant flowers to honor Matthew's memory and also remind myself of this truth. Each time I plant a seed or press a flower bulb in the cool damp soil, I remember him and remind myself of this truth. The seed is transformed through death. It must first die, and then it bursts into bloom or fruitfulness.

As the seed is planted and transformed by its death to burst into blooms and fruitfulness, so it happens with us in death—so it happened with Matthew. His earthly shell went into the ground in the cemetery at the top of the hill between two walnut trees. However, our precious Matthew was delivered from the broken body that plagued him the moment he passed. He is now transformed, and bursting with health and vitality. He is more alive, and free than he could ever be here on earth.

In the spring, following Matthew's passing, we planted a tree in our backyard in his honor—we call it "The Matthew Tree." There it stands as an ever-present reminder of his memory among us—a silent, yet palpable reminder that Matthew was here, and now he is with our Lord. It was eleven years ago when Mark and Luke dug the hole and planted that tree, which was little more than a leafless stick. The tree that began as a leafless stick has grown into a towering verdant monument in summer that bronzes into bittersweet red just in time for the boys' birthday. Luke, too, has grown from an adolescent bearing more than his share of grown-up grief into a tender-hearted, scholarly young man with wisdom only great loss can bring. As "The Matthew Tree" has become part of the landscape of our backyard, so our massive loss has become part of our family's story, and none of us will ever be the same again. One does not walk away from such a journey unscathed. Our painful soul wounds and knobbly scars are part of us now, and the Healer of our brokenness draws each of us forward into the new journey of healing from massive loss. He draws us each forward at our own pace and in His own way. He cares too deeply to leave us bleeding out alone. As we lift our wounded souls to the healing balm of His lovingkindness and submit to His ways, His mercy is great and His grace for us is immeasurable.

Crocus blossoms have always amazed me. They are the heralds of springtime. They are the brave ones, stabbing their bright green blades through the melting snow and thereby announcing that spring has once again wrenched free from winter's icy grasp. Life has burst free from the clutches of death—life always wins! One autumn afternoon, I ventured to our local garden center seeking crocus bulbs to plant in Matthew's honor. It was a day heavy with the pain of loss, and I moved slowly, aimlessly about the wooden crates holding various varieties of onion-like bulbs. A clerk approached me, eyeing me curiously.

"I'm looking for crocus bulbs," I said flatly. She nodded and reached into a nearby bin, producing a small bulb. She pressed the crinkly brown crocus bulb into my hand. Peeking from its top was a whitish-green shoot—life bursting from what seemed lifeless and without hope. How fitting that glorious life was bursting from the drab, brown lump! The image amazed me and echoed the promise of new life and resurrection. That crocus bulb became the symbol of my new journey. I had already decided to honor Matthew's memory with flowers, and now I silently vowed to honor Matthew's life with a profusion of crocus blossoms—especially crocus blossoms, and so remind myself that out of death bursts new and glorious life.

On Matthew's birthday, I planted crocus bulbs in his honor. Early each spring, their bright green blades jab through the slushy snow and burst into bloom in the sunlight. Beside my doorstep, they raise their golden trumpets and announce to this brutal world that death does not win. Just as the crocuses are first to announce that spring has burst forth once again, so they remind me that life triumphs over death. Despite the pain, the blessed truth remains, that now, Matthew is more alive, and free, than his best day on earth. Our joyful reunion on the banks of the beautiful river is just as sure as the return of spring.

FOOD FOR THOUGHT:

1. Have you experienced deep loss? How has God carried you through the indescribable pain? How has Scripture been your bedrock?

2. How has He tenderly led you forward toward healing? Does healing from massive loss even feel possible now? What would healing look like for you?

AUTHOR'S NOTE:

A t this writing, it has been eleven years since we laid Matthew's body to rest on the hill between two walnut trees. Eleven winters bleak and cold, where stinging wind and sleet have pelted me as I lay prostrate on his grave, my body heaving with the abject weeping well-known to the recently bereaved.

Eleven winters of kneeling in the snow beside his marker where the stark reality is written in stone. Two dates are carved there: the day when my life changed forever as I watched Matthew squirm beneath his oxygen mask, moments after his birth. The second date marks the wee hours of that January morning when my life was drastically altered once again—the night our family gathered together for the final time on this side of Heaven. That night we held Matthew's hands as we walked with him as far as we could into the churning black water, lifting him upon the strains of the hymns he loved, our voices trembling with sorrow. However, by faith, we know the songs of the redeemed from beyond the churning black water called him homeward with golden strains full of glorious harmony more beautiful than any hymn I sang over him.

Eleven winters of brutal reality have blown in, pummeling my wounded soul, heavy with Matthew's absence—eleven winters where the bleak frozen landscape outside mirrored the gray and brown world within. Yet greater still are the eleven years of burgeoning hope—true and living hope fueled by the truth of Scripture. Eleven years of standing firmly—defiantly upon the truth, singing out the blessed truth through streaming tears, and lifting my trembling hands to Him in worship.

Reality punches hard, yet the truth of our blessed hope towers over the stark facts—though the cruel realities often pummel us and mock our pain, it does not have the final word. Truth has the final word, and the truth is our blessed hope is firmly anchored to The Rock of Ages, it remains as fixed and unmovable as God Himself.

Eleven winters have melted away as the first emerald crocus blades stab through the slushy snow. Eleven springs have burst into bloom. At one turn, the change of season jabbed my wounded soul by having the audacity to go on as usual when my world had seemingly ended. At the other turn, I rejoiced at the daffodils raising their golden trumpets in defiance alongside the crocuses, as winter's icy grip melted away in the afternoon sun. "Life wins; death does not have the final say!" they trumpeted. The tulips lifted their shimmering scarlet cups overflowing with the truth of our blessed hope—the dry brown bulb that rested in the cold soil all winter, now burst forth in its glorious new form—our blessed hope in bloom upon my doorstep.

Eleven gardens have been planted; I've cut the furrows deep in the soft brown soil, dropped in the smooth seeds, and patted the warm earth over them with the words of the Apostle Paul repeating in my head: "What you sow does not come to life unless it dies... so it is with the resurrection from the dead. It is sown in dishonor; it is raised in glory." As I planted the seed in the soil, so Matthew's body was "planted," and as the first sprouts popped through the soil, unfolding their leaves in the afternoon sun, my heart ached for my sweet Matthew. I longed to know—to see him unfettered by special needs and seizures, his tongue loosed and dark eyes dancing with vibrant life.

Eleven summers have come and gone—summers heavy with memories of the long afternoons we spent together. Afternoons where Matthew struggled through seizures—and our final summer together as I sang for him day after day as we watched the hummingbirds dance around the feeder outside the window. The first summer without him landed hard; Mark was away at work and Luke was away at summer camps—I was alone. Alone with the silence, and the walls that seemed to continually whisper his name, and alone with the pain.

As is my custom when thoughts run helter-skelter over themselves in my mind, I write. So, one hot afternoon, I sat down at the kitchen table with my laptop and began to write Matthew's story while the details were fresh—even raw—in my memory. Day after day I wrote out the story through tears and raspy sobs. It was painful, yet cathartic. As the summer faded and the new school year ramped up, Matthew's story lay in disjointed form in my laptop.

Eleven back-to-school seasons have come and gone; reality slaps me hard each time I see his yellow school bus in our neighborhood picking up his former classmates. I often reel in pain and confusion, but the strong hands of truth grasp my shoulders and in a steady whisper say, "He doesn't need that bus anymore—no bus harness, no crash helmet, no special needs school—he's home with Me, and completely safe."

Eleven Octobers has swept in with their brisk winds that swirl the crunching leaves beneath my feet. Eleven autumns, ubiquitous with pumpkins, reminding me of my two Precious Pumpkins—the sweet and silly endearment by which I called the boys since their birth in late October. Eleven birthdays, weighty with Matthew's absence, have come and gone. I've worked hard to celebrate Luke and honor Matthew's memory.

With each passing birthday, Luke has transformed from a strapping middle-schooler in football gear blocking tackles on the offensive line, into the high school graduate smiling for photos in his cap and gown in front of the Matthew tree. Luke is now a serious-minded and scholarly man of faith and science. When he visits Mark and me, he still sits in the same spot he's always sat since he was a sun-bronzed school boy. He often sat in that spot slurping down massive slabs of watermelon on a sticky summer evening. As I look across the table at my son, now a fully-bearded young man, my mind's eye flits back to the dark-haired baby with rose-bud lips and beautiful skin. I wonder where my Jesus will take him, and what plans He has for my son. I wonder what He will do with the prayers I prayed for him since before he and Matthew were born. I wonder what Jesus will do with the hymns I sang over the boys since they were two bean-shaped circles in their sonogram picture on my fridge–with the Bible stories read and Scriptures memorized each evening in the stream of light from the hallway.

Mark and I have struggled; any imperfect man and woman wedded for life will struggle. However, the set of facts and statistics stacked against us have been daunting at best—insurmountable at times. Most couples parenting a special needs child do not survive. Many couples who lose a child in death do not survive. Yet, through God's hand upon us, and sheer tenacity, we continue to defy the harsh realities and statistics stacked against us. This coming spring we will celebrate thirty years of marriage together.

Quietly and steadily, Mark continues to work hard, providing for our family. He sometimes slips silently away to the hillside between the two walnut trees where we laid Matthew's body to rest. He honors and mourns Matthew there. It is not uncommon for me to find a small bouquet of white roses perched in a vase on our kitchen table. He often snips them for me from the rose bush we planted in Matthew's honor as he completes his mowing chores.

One Christmas morning after Matthew's passing, Mark handed me a shiny gold box. I eased off the lid, lifting off a square of cotton batting. Beneath the batting lay an antique ivory rose brooch with a shimmering gold stem. I wear it with honor as a silent testament to the journey I have walked, and the grave loss I have borne. I also wear it as a reminder of Mark's quiet, yet constant love for me. We've walked a life-altering journey that few couples survive. For that, I am humbled and grateful.

One early spring afternoon just after Matthew passed, Luke and a friend sat on our front porch after school. A thought dropped into my mind: "Make them a pizza!" So, I stepped through the fog and soul-pain of grief, got out a bowl and spoon, and set to work. Soon, I pulled a fresh pizza from my oven. As the pizza crust crunched beneath the blade I thought, "This is nuts. What am I doing?" Nonetheless, I carried the fresh pizza out to the boys, offered it to them with a brief explanation and a smile, and walked away.

However odd it seemed, that act opened the doorway to several years of investment in Luke and his posse of rowdy middle school boys. Each Wednesday evening, I began driving the boys to church youth group. As I drove my route, picking up each boy, the air in the van became increasingly heavy with the fumes of Axe body spray and middle school boy funk. I simply cracked my window, and carried on!

As Luke and his posse played Hantis or GaGa ball during rec

time after worship, I found a quiet corner of the church lobby. I pulled a notebook and pen from my purse, and wrote. I wrote about Matthew, about my grief, about the daily trials of raising Luke, and about helping him navigate and process life without Matthew. As the youth pastor and frazzled volunteers switched out the lights in the student rec center, the boys emerged with the raucous chatter and horseplay typical of middle school boys, their faces and hair damp with sweat. They all packed into my van, layering their sweaty aroma atop the lingering fumes of Axe body spray. I accounted for everyone and cracked my window further for our rowdy ride home.

As Luke progressed through Boy Scouts, I found a quiet nook in a different church lobby, pulled out my notebook and pen, and continued writing—writing out the grief, the pain, and the gaping empty hole in my life, in my time, and in my broken and bleeding soul. The pain flowed through the pen as I wrote, and the words took shape as I began to weave together this beautiful story.

I continued to invest in Luke and his posse of now high school boys. The old wives' adage says, "The route to a man's heart is through his stomach!" and it had proved itself true since I was a farmgirl at home in the kitchen and throughout my years as a wife and boy-mom. The leader of Luke's home group Bible study asked me to provide food for the group of boys. I was delighted to have the opportunity to put my kitchen skills to work as a point of entry and influence in the lives of fifteen high school boys.

My Sunday afternoons became marathon baking and cooking sessions as I prepped for Sunday evening home group. Luke and Mark helped me load the van with crockpots of nacho cheese dip, pans of brownies, and platters of cheese, crackers, fruit, and veggies. The boys met me, eager to help and see what I brought them each week. Some boys only came for the food, but in the process, heard about Jesus. The same boys who had piled into my van as sweaty middle schoolers welcomed me in, and let me pour truth into them. Some came to Christ and invited me to join them in the lake at summer camp as they were baptized. My feet swished in the gritty mud as I stood chest-deep in the lake, yet my heart was full and rejoicing. If I'd played a small part at all in this moment, I was humbled and grateful.

All the busyness, all the serving and pouring into others was time well-spent— and it was time sensitive. Never again would Luke be a high schooler with friends that allowed me to pour truth into them for the small price of feeding them. It was an open door of opportunity—open only for a little while, and I must seize that moment. However, those of us who love to serve others will pour out our last drop of strength for them and count it a joy and blessing. So it was for me.

My broken heart required the tender triage of a well-trained and compassionate listener. I made the inquiries at the church office, and Jesus brought me the kind listener I needed. During our weekly visits, I told her my story again and again. She urged me to keep writing it. She patiently listened and asked deep questions. One afternoon, I mentioned to her that I never went into Matthew's room. In the same breath, I mentioned the Scripture verse from Hosea 2:15: *".. and I will make the valley of Achor (trouble or suffering) a door of hope. . ."*

My friend reached across the table and took my hand, her eyes bright and intense: "You know what you must do, right?" she asked. I nodded. I must re-enter Matthew's room, take the first step toward reclaiming that valley of suffering, and let Him make it my door of hope. I must transform Matthew's bedroom—the room where he died—into my writing space. From that writing space, I would tell Matthew's story—the story taking shape on my laptop and within those dog-eared notebooks.

The following day, I pushed open the door and stepped into Matthew's bedroom. His bed still stood as it had been. The blue chair remained as it had been since the hospice nurse sat there recording Matthew's final moments. His beloved blue blanket was spread on his bed and his well-worn blue crash helmet lay upon his pillow—a silver cross lapel pin glistened in the dim light. Luke had pushed it into the front of Matthew's crash helmet the day after he died. Luke also gently and solemnly placed the crash helmet on Matthew's pillow, and it remained there. All was still, quiet in the dim light. I knew what I must do. I retrieved my tattered notebook and a pen, and with purposeful intent, went back into his room, sat down on the floor in front of his window, and began to write. I wrote out the pain, the grief, the tears and tangled thoughts, the fear of his memory slipping away—that I would lose him forever if I couldn't remember the soft brush of his hair, the fall of his dark eyelashes and the feel of him plopping into my lap. I knew I must reclaim the space at that moment in time—while I was still brave enough to do it.

Day after day, I took my notebook and pen, sat in the soft light near Matthew's bedroom window, and began to compose his story. As I passed through his doorway, day after day, I repeated the words of Hosea 2 and verse 15 to myself: ". . .and I will make the Valley of Achor (trouble or suffering) a door of hope.." I said it as a prayer of faith—though the pain of my trek through the valley of suffering weighed heavily upon me, I leaned forward in faith, grasping for the truth of Scripture: "Weeping may remain for the night," the psalmist said, ". . . but joy comes in the morning." The truth promised that my weeping would end, and joy and gladness would return. I reached for that hope-filled truth as day after day I wrote Matthew's story, trusting Him to reclaim my valley of suffering as my doorway to hope.

Eleven seasons have come and gone since that winter night when Matthew flew away to Jesus, and here I sit in his room completing the story that began to take shape years ago in those dog-eared notebooks. My desk sits beside his window where I used to sit on the floor and write. As I sit here writing his story, my gaze often falls to that precious place across the room where Matthew's spirit flew to Jesus and the broken body that plagued him remained behind. I ache with longing to see him now, to throw my arms about him and listen as he tells his story from his perspective and in his own voice—and so I shall, one glorious day. I still write in Matthew's room because this valley of suffering shall become a door of hope for me if I continue to follow the lead of my beautiful Jesus, who has walked with me our entire journey.

Later this month, I will drive to our local garden center and pour a scoop of dry crocus bulbs into a brown paper sack and take them home to plant on the boys' late October birthday. As I do so, I will do two things at the same time. I will honor Matthew's memory once again as I press the small, onion-like bulbs into the soil. I will also remind myself once again of this truth, as I have countless times before: the seed in the soil is released to its true glory by its death. As I press the bulb into the soil, I remember once again how Matthew's body is like a planted seed; he is now bursting with life and vibrant health on glory's side.

As I've done many times before, by faith, I will stand on tip-toe once again, peering over the horizon as far as I can see into eternity. There I know Matthew is basking in Jesus's presence, and singing in full-throated praise alongside his earthly siblings–the ones I never knew, but who now, are perhaps Matthew's old friends. As I pat the soil over the bulbs, I will likely squint away the stinging tears–the tears that tell the story of pain–pain of watching Matthew suffer for years, pain of losing him in death, and the current pain of our separation. I will cast a wistful gaze toward the stunningly blue October sky as I imagine the day–the day I cross the churning black water myself and run into the arms of my beautiful Jesus. Perhaps He will walk me to the place where Matthew awaits my arrival; perhaps Matthew will introduce me to the babies I never knew but prayed for just the same.

The sun-bronzed farmgirl in her orange sundress will loop her arm through mine as we stand together in the crisp autumn afternoon. There we will lift our crushed dreams to our Heavenly Father as a fragrant offering—an offering arising from that fertile soil of trusting surrender and true and living hope. For when our Lord crushes something, it is not to destroy it. He crushes to make new, to give new life–to resurrect, so He has done with me. The journey has crushed me, yet by His crushing, He is making something new as the seed is crushed to release its intended beauty and productivity, so the girlhood dream has been crushed in His hand. There it remains, resting in that fertile space where He does His best work– the precious place of trusting surrender and burgeoning hope.

After I complete my memorial bulb-planting, I will physically do what I must do in a greater sense for the rest of my life: I will wait. However, I wait in hope; I wait until the early days of spring for the first sign of emerald crocus blades poking through the snow. In a larger sense, I will wait in hope for the day I see my beautiful Jesus face-to-face, and when I am reunited with my precious Matthew, and the babies I never knew. Until that day, I will do what I've been doing all along. I will continue to follow my Jesus. He has proven himself more than worthy of my complete and total trust on this life changing journey–this journey that I would never have chosen on my own. I will stay in the Scriptures for they reveal more of Him to me; they are alive with His Spirit. I echo the words of the Apostle Peter, "Lord, to whom shall we go? You have the words of life, . . ." I will continue my ongoing conversation with Jesus in prayer and continue to pour out my heart to Him day after day.

I will keep telling the story of how cultivating trust in God as a young mom was the catalyst that began my search for the truth, for Who He truly is and what He truly promises. It all started with learning to trust Him, learning Him through Scripture and finding Him the all-powerful and compassionate Guide on my journey—a journey through heartbreak and a journey through loss. However, it was a deeper journey—it was a journey to the end of myself and my own strivings; it was a journey to finding His strength in my weakness and confusion, it was a journey to authenticity. It was a journey to the end of my religiosity and into intimate friendship with the Lord of All Creation—and I will never be the same again.

www.ingramcontent.com/pod-product-compliance
Lightning Source LLC
Chambersburg PA
CBHW031459120626
46545CB00005B/1671

* 9 7 9 8 8 9 1 8 5 1 6 4 1 *